HUMAN first,

LEADER second

HUMAN first,

How Self-Compassion
Outperforms Self-Criticism

LEADER second

Massimo Backus

Berrett–Koehler Publishers, Inc.

Berrett-Koehler Publishers, Inc.
1333 Broadway, Suite P100, Oakland, CA 94612-1921
Tel: (510) 817-2277; Fax: (510) 817-2278
bkconnection.com

ORDERING INFORMATION

Quantity sales. Special discounts are available on quantity purchases by corporations, associations, and others. For details, please go to bkconnection.com to see our bulk discounts or contact bookorders@bkpub.com for more information.

Individual sales. Berrett-Koehler publications are available through most bookstores. They can also be ordered directly from Berrett-Koehler: Tel: (800) 929-2929; Fax: (802) 864-7626; bkconnection.com.

Orders for college textbook / course adoption use. Please contact Berrett-Koehler: Tel: (800) 929-2929; Fax: (802) 864-7626.

Distributed to the US trade and internationally by Penguin Random House Publisher Services.

Berrett-Koehler and the BK logo are registered trademarks of Berrett-Koehler Publishers, Inc.

Printed in Canada

Berrett-Koehler books are printed on long-lasting acid-free paper. When it is available, we choose paper that has been manufactured by environmentally responsible processes. These may include using trees grown in sustainable forests, incorporating recycled paper, minimizing chlorine in bleaching, or recycling the energy produced at the paper mill.

Library of Congress Cataloging-in-Publication Data

Names: Backus, Massimo, author.
Title: Human first, leader second : how self-compassion outperforms self-criticism / Massimo Backus.
Description: First edition. | Oakland, CA : Berrett-Koehler Publishers, Inc., [2024] | Includes bibliographical references and index.
Identifiers: LCCN 2024007124 (print) | LCCN 2024007125 (ebook) | ISBN 9781523007059 (paperback) | ISBN 9781523007066 (pdf) | ISBN 9781523007073 (epub)
Subjects: LCSH: Leadership. | Self-consciousness (Awareness) | Self-actualization (Psychology) | Work-life balance. | Quality of life.
Classification: LCC HD57.7 .B3227 2024 (print) | LCC HD57.7 (ebook) | DDC 658.4/092—dc23/eng/20240424
LC record available at https://lccn.loc.gov/2024007124
LC ebook record available at https://lccn.loc.gov/2024007125

FIRST EDITION

32 31 30 29 28 27 26 25 24   »   10 9 8 7 6 5 4 3 2 1

Book production: BookMatters; Cover design: Ashley Ingram

To my Nona Rose Chimo:

May your unwavering commitment

to believing in the miraculous power

of the love we cannot see

be an inspiration to us all.

To you, the reader: You are enough.

CONTENTS

INTRODUCTION
Befriending Your Inner Asshole

In 2004 Dan Harris, a well-known ABC news anchorman for two decades, had a panic attack on live TV. Up until then, he'd been described as a gifted, intelligent, driven professional, but also as an authoritarian diva, cold and guarded.[1]

In the wake of his inferno of unease, Harris submitted to a comprehensive performance evaluation, called a 360 assessment, that included in-depth feedback from supervisors, direct reports, colleagues, and even friends and family members. The responses were so harsh that while he and his wife were reviewing the report, she had to take a break to go cry in the bathroom. Harris explained in a TED Talk that the most painful part was realizing that the aspects of his personality he was most ashamed of and had tried the hardest to hide were on full display for everyone to see: anger and self-centeredness.

Meditation had helped, but he "clearly retained the capacity to be a schmuck." Devastated by the feedback, he committed to psychotherapy, communications coaching, bias training, and couples counseling in addition to his meditation practice. Finally, when nothing seemed to make a real difference, Harris embarked on a nine-day silent retreat to practice loving-kindness meditation, which he admitted sounded like "Valentine's Day with a gun to [his] head." He'd become something of an anti-fluff meditation guru by that point, adding snark and plenty of f-bombs to his meditation teachings, attracting like-minded skeptics with his countercultural approach.

Now, he found himself on a retreat with a meditation teacher instructing him that the way to be kinder to others was to first be kinder to himself. She suggested whenever he found anger and self-centeredness creeping in, he should place his hand on his heart and say "It's okay, sweetie. I'm here for you." Harris gave it an immediate hard pass, dismissing the practice as akin to the hollow mantras of Instagram influencers and spin instructors. During meditation, instead of trying out the self-compassion practice his teacher recommended, he continued to wrestle with his "twin demons" of anger and self-centeredness. In his head, he was busy writing expletive-laden speeches to his boss complaining about promotions he deserved and never received and creating imaginary five-star Amazon reviews for his own books, all while relentlessly berating himself over how incurably self-obsessed he was. Harris was miserable.

Halfway into the retreat, mid-meditation, he finally caved, placing a hand on his heart, and telling himself "It's all good, dude. I know this sucks, but I've got you." While he felt awkward and embarrassed, he realized in that moment that self-compassion wasn't weak or indulgent but instead "radical disarmament." By refusing to fight his demons and seeing them as what I call well-intentioned, misinformed protectors (WIMPs), he weakened their power over him.

Only once we realize that we are human first, not [insert your fancy job title], can we face the deep work of self-compassion. The godmother of self-compassion, author Kristin Neff, has encouraged us for well over a decade to embrace our common humanity with mindfulness and self-kindness.[2] Being able to hold your heart and connect to your humanity is the foundation of every other endeavor, including leadership. When harnessed properly, self-compassionate leadership can empower individuals, teams, and organizations to foster cultures of excellence through awareness, acceptance, and accountability.

WHAT IS SELF-COMPASSIONATE LEADERSHIP?

I define self-compassionate leadership as nonjudgmental awareness of our internal states, empathetic acceptance of our imperfect humanity, and thoughtful accountability for leading ourselves and others.

Harris spoke to the same point when he said, "a lack of love ... is at the root of our most pressing problems, from inequality to violence to the climate crisis. Obviously, these are all massive problems that are going to require massive structural change, but at a baseline, they also require us to care about one another. And it is harder to do that when you're stuck in a ceaseless spiral of self-centered self-flagellation."

If you just rolled your eyes and audibly sighed, I get it.

I've come to the topic of self-compassionate leadership only after many decades and detours. I struggled throughout my school years and during the first few years of college. Dyslexia and the need to cope with a learning difference in traditional educational settings shaped much of my early life experience. I was unfit for the traditional educational system, which led me to question my intellect, abilities, and worth from a young age. I attended seven universities and dropped out once for an extended break before graduating with a master's degree in organizational behavioral psychology from Claremont Graduate University in Southern California.

I don't have it all figured out. Rather, I've found something that has fundamentally changed my life and the lives of thousands of leaders I've worked with as an executive coach. I know I'm not alone in the struggles and challenges that leadership brings. I hope what I learned can benefit you in the profound way it has impacted me.

My fifteen-plus years of experience in talent development and leadership coaching have given me a front-row seat to observe company cultures in the US, UK, and Canada while working with 3,000 emerging and seasoned leaders in mid-size and Fortune 500 companies. In one-on-one conversations, group coaching sessions, and workshops, I gathered data on what stands in the way of effective leadership, how the stories we tell ourselves limit our capacity, and how we can create cultures of trust by first learning to trust ourselves. I combine that practical experience with the latest research on leadership development and behavioral science to teach leaders like you how to transform old habits and dysfunctional patterns holding you back so you can uncover who you really are and who you want to be.

As the saying goes, "change happens when the pain of staying the same is greater than the pain of change." It took Harris decades. It took me decades. How about you? What led you to pick up this book, even though the mention of self-compassion induces an involuntary cringe in so many high-performing leaders like you? When it comes to work, we're often concerned that self-compassion will kill our motivation, dull our competitive edge, and make us weak, complacent, or prone to self-pity. The opposite is true.

Compassion is a feeling of deep empathy and concern for the well-being of others paired with a strong desire to help. As Harris says in his TED Talk, "Self-love, properly understood not as narcissism but as having your own back, is not selfish. It makes you better at loving other people." Most of us consider loving and caring about other people an important virtue of living in human society, yet we scoff at directing the same principle toward ourselves and in turn toward our approach to leadership. Even though most of us want and value love and genuine care, we somehow exclude this value from how we run organizations, lead teams, or build societies.

Research by Laura Barnard and John Curry at Duke University shows the practice of self-compassion leads to higher levels of life satisfaction, happiness, self-confidence, optimism, curiosity, creativity, and gratitude.[3] People who are compassionate toward themselves are better at seeing failure as a learning opportunity and maintaining motivation in the face of adversity. Ask yourself: wouldn't that be a big plus in your personal and professional life? Barnard and Curry found that self-compassion decreased anxiety, depression, stress, rumination, perfectionism, and fear of failure.[4] Now do you see the cost-benefit ratio?

It's time to move on from the antiquated leadership philosophy that we must suffer to succeed. Struggles are certainly a part of life. However, self-compassionate leadership allows us to ease our own suffering so we can alleviate it in others and better serve the people we lead. If "suffering" sounds too dramatic to you, feel free to swap it out for "discomfort" or "challenge." No matter what you call it, the point is that in times of crisis the metaphor of putting on your own oxygen mask before helping others is so popular because it's true.

And yet when I first learned about self-compassion, I was skeptical.

Many books and resources about this topic are full of excellent content, yet I found myself turned off by the fluffy, pastel-colored branding and platitudinous tone. Although I gravitated toward the concept of self-compassion, I didn't see myself as the intended audience. For me, self-compassion is not hugging myself and talking to my inner child but rather developing an experimental, deliberate practice to experience my full humanity without judgment.

Similarly, there's an overwhelming amount of content out there about leadership development. New ideas, philosophies, and approaches are published every year. You could spend a lifetime watching TED Talks, listening to leadership podcasts, and attending the newest training or workshop. Few have stood the test of time.

WHY THIS BOOK?

I had a hunch that self-compassion could bridge the gap between my personal and professional persona, my humanity, and my leadership work. However, I found few resources about the fusion of self-compassion and leadership practice. Even though research suggests clear benefits to embracing self-compassion, it has yet to catch on in organizational culture, leadership, and management best practices. That's why I wrote this book.

The Hoffman Process, an eight-day intensive personal development retreat that I attended in Northern California, forever changed my most important relationship—my relationship with myself. The experience of learning to love myself inspired me to research my hypothesis for this book: self-compassion is the greatest untapped resource for transformative leadership.

The Hoffman Process created a massive shift in the way I love and lead, so I wrote the book I needed to fully integrate self-compassion into my life and leadership work. I'm distilling the work of scholars, scientists, and thought leaders in the field of self-compassion to make it accessible and applicable to leaders everywhere.

Too often, leadership and the authority, status, and power that come with it cause deep issues, both within us and interpersonally. Leaders may lose sight of both their own and others' humanity. They may become ultracompetitive, get caught up in their own hype, feel superior to their direct reports, and express it with a lack of compassion and empathy, even coldness and cruelty. This kind of leader often feels incredibly lonely, detached, and closed off. They may be burned out because they're trying to be all things to all people. They may think they'll never be good enough and are overcompensating to prove themselves. Or they may have limited awareness that their leadership approach isn't working but don't know what to change or how to begin, pushing them toward perfectionism, imposter syndrome, or high stress and anxiety. These leaders may be overly demanding of themselves and others, undervaluing colleagues, micromanaging their team, or leading from a place of fear.

IS THIS BOOK FOR YOU?

This book is for leaders who have felt as stuck as I have—driven more by fear than by purpose, guided by the validation of others rather than appreciation for oneself. It's for those of us who always look toward the next promotion to justify all the late nights rather than finding balance between purposeful work and rest. This book is for leaders hiding behind masks but only fooling themselves, constantly plagued by imposter syndrome and self-doubt. It's for those of us who've falsely believed titles, access, and influence give us power, only to realize we've given away our power.

There is no blueprint, silver bullet, or playbook for leadership development that works for every person in every situation, and I'm not advocating for implementing self-compassion to the exclusion of all else. However, I've found that self-compassion can offer a cluster of ideas, behaviors, and activities that act as coordinates to help us orient ourselves and bring us back to center when we get lost. Self-compassion is the equivalent of the big red arrow on the map denoting: you are here. It gives us the starting point at every moment of our lives.

Standing where we are, inhabiting whatever space we're in, physically and emotionally, is the necessary first step that we often forget. From here, we can use self-compassion to choose new tools and resources, allowing our self-awareness to illuminate the dark like a flashlight, our purpose to guide our direction like a compass, and our values to suggest our route like a map.

WHAT THIS BOOK CAN DO FOR YOU

While doing this work, I realized my own blocks to being an effective leader. All my expertise, capabilities, and confidence couldn't mask my challenges leading my own teams. Like so many leaders I worked with, I struggled with feelings of never being good enough. If I made a mistake, I beat myself up instead of offering myself kindness. I tried even harder, white-knuckled it, and became more rigid. Feedback made me defensive, so I closed myself off to different ideas or doubled down on my own, which only made everything worse. Slowly, I learned to take a step back and find a gentler, more flexible approach.

Harris had a similar experience, finally embracing self-compassion as the countercultural approach to "the never-enough-ness and always-behind-ness that society . . . wants us to feel. It's courageous because it's hard to look at your demons. And it's happiness-producing because when you high-five your demons, they don't own you as much. And all of that makes you more generous and more available. If that sounds grandiose or touchy-feely to you, let me put it to you another

way: the view is so much better when you pull your head out
of your ass."

This book offers an actionable, experimental resource for
leaders to increase their personal and professional quality of
life. You're not a leader trying to be human. You are a human
first, trying to lead other humans. As we hear more and more
often, there are no hard and soft skills, only human and technical skills. This book will help you exponentially grow your
human skills while fostering the resilience and curiosity you
need to bolster your technical skills. There is no secret sauce
that's already bottled and ready to be bought. Each of us needs
to make our own secret sauce, and that takes a lifetime.

I will introduce you to the Ward Model—the self-
compassionate leadership framework I've created to help you
break free from cycles of emotions, thoughts, and behaviors
that keep you stuck, burn you out, and prevent you from living a life aligned with your core values and vision. The Ward
Model allows you to become aware of what's happening inside and around you at any given moment, accept your complex humanity without judgment, and be accountable for the
next intentional step you take and, ultimately, how you show
up in your life.

This book is less "prescriptive inspirational quote over
heavily filtered mountaintop picture" and more "you and me
in the kitchen tweaking the recipe together and taste testing
as we go." In short, I won't tell you what to do, but I'll help
you discover what you already know deep down. In every
chapter, you will find real-world examples, questions for
self-discovery, and practical exercises to apply the concepts of
self-compassionate leadership.

Inspirational self-help books and motivational one-liners have rarely worked for me in a lasting and sustainable way. If they're your thing, that's great. There are a lot of resources already out there for you. But if that's not you, keep reading. Throughout the book, I include case studies I call "Woo-Woo Wins" as a nod to my formerly cynical self. To protect the privacy of the clients I've had the privilege of coaching, the names in many of the stories in this book have been changed. If you too look at self-compassion with an involuntary eye roll, these practical examples of how my clients, friends, and colleagues forever changed the way they live and lead might offer you a new perspective. My own cynicism was a response mechanism to distance myself from something that, at face value, seems impractical but is actually the most important work of my life. I invite you to be curious about these "Woo-Woo Wins" whenever you come across them in these pages. Remember, we're in the kitchen cooking together, so allow yourself to be surprised by what tastes or feels good.

I hope this book will help you deploy self-compassion to lead with your humanity and trust that you are a work in progress—never finished, but always growing beyond who you were yesterday.

1 » THE TWO JOBS

Take Off Your Leadership Costume

> Everything worthwhile in life is won through
> surmounting the associated negative experience.
> Any attempt to escape the negative, to avoid it or
> squash it or silence it, only backfires. The avoidance
> of suffering is a form of suffering. The avoidance of
> struggle is a struggle. The denial of failure is failure.
> Hiding what is shameful is itself a form of shame.
>
> MARK MANSON, *The Subtle Art of Not Giving a F*ck*

"Mass, you're the best facilitator we've ever seen." As the head of global leadership development at Slalom Consulting, an international business and technology consulting firm, I traveled across the United States, collaborating with some of the brightest leaders in our organization. Many people praised my facilitation skills, often referring to me as a "sage on the stage." I was privileged to witness their growth and development firsthand. It was easy to get caught up in the admiration and mistakenly claim their progress as my own.

In my pursuit to enhance my skills, I voluntarily participated in a 360 assessment just like Dan Harris, whose story I shared in the introduction. This evaluation tool is well known for its harsh but honest feedback. Despite the accolades and recognition I received while on the job, the assessment painted a starkly different picture. The results clearly labeled me as an ineffective manager. The person responsible for growing all the leaders in the organization was objectively a bad leader. The irony was (almost) funny. Feedback highlighted my controlling and defensive demeanor, with one courageous employee even describing me as a bully.

I was devastated. The feedback felt like a savage punch to the gut, making me feel like I was about to throw up. So I did what any logical person would do—I defended myself: I'm not defensive. You're defensive for saying that I'm defensive. I was completely oblivious to how incredibly defensive my defense sounded. That's how shockingly unaware I was. At some level, I knew they were right, but it seemed almost impossible for me to process. I struggled to reconcile the image people had of me with my self-perception. Immediately, I went into problem-solving mode. I was a leadership expert. I could fix this!

I was committed to leveraging the skills and tools I used to help others grow and apply them to myself. I had the best intentions. I tried so hard. For months. When I was called in for a follow-up conversation with my manager six months later, I was cautiously hopeful. I thought she was going to say: "You've made a lot of progress. We're really proud of you." She didn't. My manager acknowledged my genuine attempts to change but emphasized that it hadn't translated into a perceptible improvement in the team dynamics. Instead, she told me the team felt the same way about me as they had six months before. I felt crushed all over again. I was trying as hard as I could without making significant progress.

Even if our backgrounds and specific situations are different, maybe you can relate. Have you ever felt like this?

» I'm the only one struggling with this challenge.

» I need to be the smartest or most dominant person in the meeting.

» Nothing I do is ever good enough.

» I feel overwhelmed by constant to-do lists and overly organized fun.

» I have to compensate for other people (finish what they started, get people to make progress, clean up after everyone).

» I constantly have to prove myself at work or in my personal life.

» I can rarely focus on anything for too long.

» I feel lonely despite being surrounded by people I love and care about.

» I expect things to go wrong and anticipate having to fix them.

» I believe, deep down, that the world is against me.

» I tend to put people into boxes and attach rigid labels.

The stories and beliefs we unquestioningly accept as true speak to our deepest fears of not being good enough. Core to our identity, they are so ingrained that it's hard to question their validity. In a threat situation—big or small, real or imagined—these core beliefs come to the "rescue" to keep us safe (or employed). But these fears and stories also cause many leaders to take on a second full-time job in addition to the already challenging position listed in their job title.

THE SECOND FULL-TIME JOB: THE SINGLE BIGGEST WASTE OF ORGANIZATIONAL RESOURCES

According to developmental psychologists Robert Kegan and Lisa Lahey, all of us are working two jobs instead of one.[5] The first job is the one we're hired to do. It's the job our companies pay us for, consisting of our duties and responsibilities, the targets and objectives we're expected to meet, and the official role we perform. But on top of that, every one of us holds a secret second job. This second job consists of the energy and time we spend hiding, masking, and pretending in an effort to cover our weaknesses and manage other people's impressions of us. It entails showing only our best side, playing politics, and hiding uncertainties, inadequacies, and limitations.

A 2014 *Harvard Business Review* article explains "covering" as behavior employees use to mask or hide certain parts of their identities, personalities, or struggles. While this behavior disproportionately affects minority groups, it impacts everyone. Authors Dorie Clark and Christie Smith report that 61 percent of employees admit to covering: "A gay person might be technically out, but not display pictures of their partner at work. A working mom might never talk about her kids, so as to appear 'serious' about her career. A straight white man—45% of whom also report covering—might keep quiet about a mental health issue he's facing."

Our drive to belong to a family, community, crew, or organization often overrides our desire to be true to ourselves. "Covering" or hiding our true identity and self is shockingly common and adversely impacts us, our peers, and our employees.

This second job was exactly what I was doing. Before the inevitable confrontation with the feedback, I'd spent years of my life and massive amounts of energy attempting to hide my challenges. The silly thing is I was doing it in plain sight. Everyone else could see it. We can often spot this behavior in others while being blind to our own charade.

Kegan and Lahey explain that people expend vast efforts "covering up their weaknesses, managing other people's impressions of them, showing themselves to their best advantage, playing politics, hiding their inadequacies, hiding their uncertainties, hiding their limitations. Hiding. We regard this as the single biggest loss of resources that organizations suffer every day. Is anything more valuable to a company than how its people spend their energies? The total cost of this waste is simple to state and staggering to contemplate: it prevents organizations and the people who work in them, from reaching their full potential."[6]

Covering is a lose-lose proposition for employees and employers alike. As an employee, you may feel as if you're living the life of a double agent, always stressed about doing the job you were hired for plus your second job of hiding your true self. Think about this: the single biggest cause of burnout is not overload but a work environment that forces a prolonged lack of personal growth. As an employer, you're missing out on the full contribution and impact your employees could make while simultaneously having to absorb the cost of their secret limitations. Kegan and Lahey remind us that we humans are just as wired for self-protection as we are for psychological growth and development. Often this urge to protect ourselves leads to rigidity and an unwillingness to change, even if our current approach causes significant damage.

If you relate to this and think you and your team are engaged in this form of hiding and self-protection, it's essential to recognize that this pattern may be a manifestation of a lack of trust and psychological safety in the work environment. It's natural to want to hide our weaknesses, and acknowledging this behavior is the first step to emerging from the shadows. We all replay outdated stories and limiting beliefs about ourselves in our heads. We listen to these inner critics, even when they're brutally judgmental, and these voices and fear-based thoughts can cause real damage. However, we often forget that they're based on good intentions and attempts to keep us safe. That's why I've coined the term "well-intentioned, misinformed protectors," or WIMPs.

WELL-INTENTIONED, MISINFORMED PROTECTORS: YOUR LEADERSHIP KRYPTONITE

We often expect leaders to be heroes with superpowers: X-ray vision to foresee problems, telepathy to understand every team member's needs, flexibility to adapt to diverse challenges, and stamina to endure relentless demands. This idealized view of leadership creates an unrealistic expectation of infallibility and invulnerability.

In the face of these expectations, our WIMPs play a critical and often misunderstood role by serving as a sort of armor, or leadership costume. I've identified six main types of WIMPs: the perfectionist, the hard-ass, the achiever, the people pleaser, the imposter, and the contrarian.

These protectors, though well intentioned, are informed by the fears and limited understanding of our younger selves. While WIMPs intend to safeguard us, their strategies are based on misconceptions about what effective leadership entails. WIMPs urge leaders to maintain a facade of perfection, seek relentless validation, and hide any sign of weakness or uncertainty to avoid perceived dangers like vulnerability, criticism, and failure. They push for an unattainable standard of superhuman performance, forcing us to stretch ourselves in unsustainable ways.

This pursuit can become our leadership kryptonite, not because human fallibility is inherently detrimental, but because denying our own limitations cuts us off from our greatest strength—our authentic humanity. WIMPs, in their effort to protect, inadvertently encourage a leadership style disconnected from the very qualities that make us relatable and effective. They foster a culture of invulnerability that undermines genuine connection and empathy, shielding leaders from embracing their true power.

GET TO KNOW YOUR WIMPS

You may have met one or several of the six WIMP personas as they emerged from your formative experiences. As complex humans, we don't fall neatly into one, or even several, of these categories of WIMPs. However, they can help us understand some of our most prominent tendencies in context.

The Perfectionist

The perfectionist seeks external validation instead of intrinsic self-worth and sets unattainable goals and expectations for themselves and everyone else. Perfectionists strive to meet their personal standard of perfection, which isn't clearly defined, so they're doomed to failure from the start. They are always chasing an elusive ideal, never reaching it, then mercilessly judging themselves for being a failure.

Perfectionists tend to be black-and-white, right-or-wrong, binary thinkers. There are no grey areas. There is no room for errors or flawed humanity. They become defensive and critical when others don't perceive them as perfect or when they judge someone else as lacking, because worth and value are tied to achieving perfection, not being human.

Core strength: The perfectionist is thorough, pays close attention to aesthetics, and produces excellence that inspires others.

Core fear: If I'm not the best, then I'm the worst and "not enough," which means I'm unworthy.

Core drivers: Superiority and protection from the judgment of others.

Catch phrases:

> » I have to win.

> » I'm not good enough.

> » If it's not perfect, then I failed.

> » If I'm not the best, then I'm the worst.

» If it's not perfect, then I didn't try hard enough.

» If it's not perfect, then I'm not good enough to do this job.

» When things are perfect, I'm in control and all is right in the world.

» I'm not unrealistic; I just have high standards and expect the best.

Low self-worth that results in perfectionism isn't always caused by extreme childhood trauma or abusive parents. You can experience critical mental chatter and perfectionism even when you've had a pretty good childhood and loving parents, as I did. Much of my personal "not-good-enough" trope originated with dyslexia in early childhood. The resources for dealing with my diagnosis were not as comprehensive and effective as they are today. For years, I struggled with feeling left out and left behind in school, and a consequent feeling of low self-worth.

As an adult, I realized the education system was not designed for my dyslexic mind and how I think and learn the best. It took me decades to understand I wasn't flawed, just different. Self-compassion helped me see that what I (and society) considered a disability was actually cognitive diversity. Today we openly talk about and value neurodiversity, but back then I never heard it framed that way and thus felt shame for an innate part of who I was. I now see the gifts embodied in this difference rather than just the ways I fell short of perfection in traditional educational structures. I was great at problem solving, connecting disparate ideas to form a cohesive argument, and coming up with unique metaphors and illustrations to express and share my thoughts. Self-compassion allowed me to see myself as neither good nor bad but as a combination of strengths, weaknesses, and unique traits. I realized I wanted and deserved love and connection. The "not-good-enough" story comes in many flavors. *I'm a failure. I'm a fuck-up. I will never get it right. What's the point? I might as well give up.* Interestingly, it often affects leaders who have already achieved a measure of success—but that success is never enough. Instead, they continue performing with a chip on their shoulder, always feeling the urge to prove themselves, never asking for help, and refusing to show any weakness. Whatever your personal story and the specific words you hear in your head, you have probably noticed that they bleed into every aspect of your life, including your career.

We can get caught up in the idea that we, as leaders, must try to be more human, as if there are certain practices that make leaders more human. The irony is blatant. We are already human; we just forget that sometimes. We are humans first, leaders second. To be human is to be imperfect and fallible and still know that we deserve love and respect. Self-compassion gives us the peace of mind that we are enough exactly as we are. We don't need to do or be anything else to access connection and kindness.

The Hard-Ass

The hard-ass is more concerned with being right than being perfect. The hard-ass has high standards, always knows best, and refuses to accept being wrong. A hard-ass is hardest on themselves and wouldn't ask anyone to do anything they aren't willing to do themselves. Relentlessly pushing their team to achieve their best, the hard-ass is focused on accomplishing tasks rather than considering how people feel in the workplace. It's business, not personal.

The saying "It's lonely at the top" resonates with the hard-ass, who sees their intensity and commitment as driving forces behind their success. The hard-ass fears losing everything they've achieved by showing their humanity, which they consider weakness. Their armor has become part of their identity. Nice guys, they believe, finish last. But at their core, hard-asses are self-protective and sensitive, with their defensiveness acting as the proverbial shell keeping the soft crab safe inside.

Core strength: The hard-ass makes confident decisions in emergency situations and leads teams through uncertain times with conviction.

Core fear: If I don't demand the best, we are at risk of worst-case scenarios. I have a fear of looking incompetent. My scarcity mindset leads me to fear losing it all, so I hold on to what has worked, which is to push myself and others relentlessly.

Core drivers: A need to control outcomes, even those outside their control; dominance; and winning at all costs.

Catch phrases:

> » It's better to be respected than liked.
> » If I'm not driving for top performance, no one will.
> » If other people can't do it right, I'll just do it on my own.
> » I push people hard because I want what's right for the company.

» I'm not intimidating; I just have high standards and expect the very best from others.

One of my past coaching clients, Max, was the CEO of a rapidly growing Bay Area technology business. Max came to this position with a strong background as a sales executive and high standards that he would communicate by yelling and demanding excellence. There was one right way to do things: his way. He was respected for his outstanding technical skills but feared for his terrible people skills. He had a hard time understanding the weight and impact of his words and how intimidating his presence was.

Scared to look bad or incompetent, Max disliked surprises and hated being put on the spot to make decisions. He had a deep need for control, leading to a fixed rather than flexible approach to problems. He lacked the curiosity to consider other people's opinions and the empathy to see anyone else's perspective. So he pushed and bulldozed and white-knuckled it.

If fear is what turns a hard-ass into a bully or a jerk, self-compassion is what gives us the courage to explore the worst parts of ourselves instead of becoming defensive and recoiling in shame. Self-compassion can alleviate the scarcity mindset that drives hard-asses and makes every situation seem high stakes, every mistake critical, and every show of weakness lethal. Self-compassion doesn't let us off the hook—it will not make a hard-ass feel better about mistreating others—but it will provide a nonjudgmental approach to discovering the root of the behavior. It teaches us how to balance self-kindness and accountability so we can call ourselves on our own shit and make lasting changes.

The Achiever

The achiever exhibits a perpetual sense of urgency, always asking, "Are we there yet?" Impatience characterizes their approach. Afflicted with an intense fear of missing out, they are constantly worried that if they're not on their game 24/7, someone younger, hungrier, and better will surpass them. Achievers proudly exclaim that they can outwork anyone.

Achievers are constantly eyeing the next promotion, next award, next accolade, next title. Successes and achievements immediately get swallowed up in the black hole that is their need for external validation. No accomplishment can ever make them feel satisfied. They don't pause to celebrate victories, instead finding temporary solace in constant productivity, industriousness, and the relentless pursuit of progress and improvement.

Core strength: The achiever will push through heavy workloads and demanding timelines to accomplish the goal.

Core fear: If I stop or slow down, I will be seen as lazy and judged as a failure.

Core drivers: The need for power and protection from the judgment of others; an insatiable black hole in need of external validation.

Catch phrases:

> » If I'm not winning, I'm losing.
> » Once this project is done, I'll take a vacation.
> » If I just had X, I'd be satisfied.
> » I'm never satisfied with my success and achievement.

» If I get this award, my boss will have to say yes to my request for a raise.

» If I'm not progressing, I'm not worthy of the position I have.

» If I got that promotion, people would finally respect me.

Achievers are programmed to believe that success is defined not only by their ability to lead but also by their attainment of constant progress and ever greater titles, authority, compensation, and accolades. They strive and fight and scrap and persevere to attain these markers of external validation—outward signs that they've been deemed worthy. Even when achievers reach the upper echelons of business, they can't relax. They must constantly prove they deserve to be there. Rise and grind! Hustle! They can fall prey to the idea that their value lies in doing rather than being. The more they do, achieve, and perform, the higher they will rise in the regard of others.

Of course, with leadership comes the need to deliver results, meet performance metrics, and hit targets. There is nothing wrong with being bold and setting ambitious goals. The problem arises when we link our intrinsic self-worth to external validation and rewards. We all know this, but it's challenging to remember when much of leadership culture encourages us to measure our value according to our job titles, the size of our teams, and our annual bonuses. Have you ever caught yourself comparing the size of your team or organization to that of a colleague or peer? Have you ever had a case of org chart envy?

Deploying self-compassion reminds us that external validation is a finger trap—the children's toy that catches your index fingers in a bamboo tube. The more you struggle and pull, the tighter you're gripped in the trap. Similarly, the more we pursue external confirmation of our internal worth and let the world dictate whether we feel like "enough," the harder it is to escape that trap. By helping us calibrate and balance the external and internal, the doing and being, self-compassion allows us to loosen our grip to escape the trap.

The People Pleaser

The people pleaser conforms, avoids conflict at all costs, manages other people's emotions, and focuses on everyone else's needs to uphold harmony. Driven by a fear of not being liked or included, upsetting others, or making situations worse, people pleasers are scared to rock the boat and tend to go along to get along. They often say "yes" when they want to say "no" and find it challenging to establish clear boundaries. They prefer to absorb any underlying tensions and stress rather than face direct conflict. Labeled as peacekeepers, servant leaders, or doormats, people pleasers place a priority on being liked rather than respected for delivering hard truths or practicing candor.

Core strength: The people pleaser creates harmony in a team fraught with conflict, naturally empathizes, and reduces friction to accomplish work.

Core fear: I fear that showing my true self or inserting my own needs or agenda will lead to rejection and abandonment.

Core drivers: Acceptance from others and the need to be liked.

Catch phrases:

» Leaders eat last.

» It's better to be liked than respected.

» Servant leadership requires self-sacrifice.

» When I know people like me, I feel safe.

» If I upset someone, I assume they no longer like me.

» If I'm not liked by everyone, my job may be at risk.

» I'm not meek; I just like harmony and try to avoid conflict.

Although we still have some outdated ideas on hard-nosed, large-and-in-charge executive leaders, recently there's been a movement toward "people-first" leadership. The people-first approach prioritizes the unique needs, strengths, and goals of employees. Not only is this approach the right thing to do but it is also necessary to successfully compete for talent. Employees have easy access to LinkedIn and Glassdoor to learn about company culture, benefits, and opportunities for promotion within their industry. Companies must attract top-level talent by focusing not simply on retention but on customized growth opportunities.

However, we're now at risk of overcorrecting. Leadership problems can afflict not only the drill sergeant but also the complacent people pleaser who always puts the needs of others first. We don't need self-aggrandizing leaders, but neither do we benefit from leaders who deny their own limitations and care for everyone else at the expense of their own health and sanity. The servant leader who says yes to all requests will eventually burn out. Have you noticed that when you're extra efficient and respond rapidly to emails, the result is never more time or space, but simply more emails? Limitless tasks, piles of work, and urgent requests will flood into any space you create, so you must set boundaries or eventually be buried under the avalanche.

Leaders who embrace their humanity with self-compassion are showing up with their armor off. Such leaders have a deep understanding of their strengths, gifts, and talents and a keen awareness of their flaws and weaknesses. Because they accept their humanity, they don't feel the need to hide any part of their whole selves, even if that means they won't be liked by everyone, will disappoint some people, or will cause occasional friction and conflict on their team. They don't bury their excellence under false humility or conceal their limitations with fake bravado. They allow themselves to be fully human, giving permission to everyone around them to do the same.

Self-compassion also protects recovering people pleasers from burnout and compassion fatigue, according to a 2020 study of healthcare professionals by Zeena Hashem and Pia Zeinoun.[7] Leadership positions in helping professions (such as therapists, medical personnel, and social workers) are often expected to constantly serve others while forgetting themselves almost entirely. Hashem and Zeinoun found that "self-compassion practices explained 22 percent of the variance in burnout" among the nurses who participated in the study. The study showed that participants who practiced self-compassion by not judging their high level of emotional exhaustion were less likely to experience burnout.

Self-compassion can be the antidote to compassion fatigue because it requires us to put on our own oxygen mask first.

The Imposter

The imposter feels undeserving of any success they've earned. Always worried about being found out for "who they really are," imposters feel like they've somehow cheated their way into whatever position they hold. They constantly minimize their abilities, lack self-confidence, and are notoriously bad at taking compliments. Their default response is self-deprecation. Because they feel inferior to other people, they rarely engage as equals with peers. Imposters often think of themselves as misfits who are missing a key ingredient or are broken in some unfixable way. Their low self-worth can hold them back from reaching bigger goals and, worse, prevent them from imagining and defining their purpose.

Core strength: The imposter is unlikely to overestimate their abilities, which makes them conscientious and prudent when taking on challenges that require new skills.

Core fear: I'll probably fail, so what's the point in trying in the first place? Failure avoided by complacency is better than failure resulting from ambition.

Core drivers: The need for protection from the judgment and rejection of others.

Catch phrases:

> » I'm a fraud and will be found out eventually.

> » If people really knew me ...

» I don't belong here and don't fit in.

» If they knew how incompetent and useless I was, I would be fired.

» I can't do this and don't understand why other people think I can.

» If I try and fail, I'm worse off than I would be if I never tried at all.

» There's something wrong with me.

When we persistently doubt our abilities and talents, feel as though we don't deserve our accolades, or haven't earned our achievements, we may experience a constant fear of being exposed for lacking talent or skill. It's easy to see how low intrinsic self-worth and the need to garner outside validation make us prone to doubt whether we really deserve praise. We quietly ask ourselves if we're just really good at faking it and dread the day everyone will finally find out who we really are—a fraud. Wondering if you belong and identifying as a misfit can lead to feeling like you're the odd one out or will never be part of the group. Once everyone else finds out who you truly are, they will reject you.

I experienced imposter syndrome while writing this book. Let's just say I had daily opportunities to practice self-compassion, which didn't erase my imposter syndrome but helped me put it in perspective. The more I practice self-compassion, the less imposter syndrome I experience. Throughout my life, I've often feared being exposed as a fraud. My résumé is proof of all the jobs I started and quit and the educational programs and universities I attended and dropped out of. My twenties were littered with false starts and career changes. I spent years trying to figure out where I belonged, where I would feel right. Self-compassion helped me understand that no external circumstances would give me the feeling of belonging. Having dyslexia was one of the main drivers of my imposter syndrome. I was privileged to have loving parents who had the means to help me with tutors and support me through academic and career ups and downs. I got chance after chance. Where I am today is due to hard work and undoubtedly a lot of luck. Many people with language-based learning differences are not as fortunate. While self-compassion can help us personally, it is also essential to remember that once we apply it to ourselves, we have greater capacity to extend it to others. We may start advocating for systemic changes that alleviate collective suffering and offer people the support they need to thrive. Because of my experience with dyslexia in the educational system and my passion for improving outcomes for the next generation, I'm deeply grateful for the opportunity to serve on the board of a Seattle-area school for students with dyslexia and other language-based learning differences, where I get to help shape supportive school policies and educational frameworks. I also had the honor of speaking to a class of eighth graders. Struggling with imposter syndrome myself, I found it meaningful to encourage them to trust their abilities and creativity while validating their struggles and inviting them to see the gifts within. Self-compassion allowed me to show up for these kids as my whole self and model that they can find their own path and make a beautiful life for themselves. It remains one of the most moving moments of my life and career.

The Contrarian

The contrarian goes against the grain, frequently playing devil's advocate and challenging norms. Contrarians habitually zig when everyone else zags. They "think differently" from everyone else—and "different," in their estimation, means "better." They're overconfident in their ideas and perspectives, considering anything new or norm-defying superior to established practices.

Contrarians seldom have the patience to advocate for their big ideas beyond initial discussions to gain consensus. Even when they express verbal agreement with others, they may hold onto contradicting viewpoints internally. If outcomes deviate from expectations, the contrarian's go-to response is "I told you so." They're quick to point out when they're right but ready to redirect focus or shift blame when proven wrong. Contrarians can be indecisive and uneasy when held accountable for specific decisions.

Core strength: The contrarian offers a big-picture vision and innovative ideas to challenge the status quo and make impossible breakthroughs possible.

Core fear: If I don't come up with exceptional ideas all the time, I will be perceived as average, which is unacceptable.

Core drivers: The need to be perceived as different, special, and visionary.

Catch phrases:

» It's better to be different than conform to what I don't understand or agree with.

» By regularly changing my opinion, I avoid being held accountable for the outcome.

» By challenging other people's ideas, I look smart.

» New is always better.

» By questioning other people's work, I don't have to come up with my own solutions.

Some highly successful entrepreneurs and company CEOs could be considered contrarians. These can be highly intelligent visionaries with eccentric streaks whose appetite for risk and novelty can skyrocket a company to a billion-dollar valuation one year and bankrupt it the next.

This impulsivity can lead companies to expedite product launches to outpace competitors while compromising quality and security. The rush often backfires, causing delays and damaging reputations. Rapid growth requires rapid recruitment, which can destabilize an organization's culture and core values, leading to increased human resources issues and costly employee training and turnover. When a charismatic contrarian heads a company or a team, it can lead to unilateral decisions that exclude key stakeholders and disregard the nuances of organizational politics, restricting future opportunities.

Self-compassion helps contrarians take a pause, making it less likely they'll break something irreparable. It helps them remember that they are both special and yet connected to others, so they'll feel less like they need to set themselves apart from the rest to maintain their uniqueness. Self-compassion can help contrarians be who they are rather than just trying to be different from the mainstream.

Comedian Jon Stewart was asked in an interview with radio host Howard Stern how long it took him to get good at stand-up. During his early career, Stewart worked at the Comedy Cellar in New York City and was regularly assigned to the last spot at 2 a.m.: "You learn how to be yourself, and once you learn how to be yourself, that's when it opens up. You learn how to channel what you actually care about, and then you find your voice."[8] Self-compassion can help leaders learn who they are at their core and what lights them up so they'll see big ideas and projects through to the end instead of abandoning them after the initial excitement wears off and the first obstacles appear. Self-compassion can alleviate the contrarian's need to be "the next big thing" and instead be their truest selves.

Our WIMPs Are Trying to Tell Us Something

If you see yourself in one or more of these well-intentioned, misinformed protectors, you may have already started mercilessly judging yourself. Our goal is to change our relationship with the WIMPs. We may think of them as our shadow or dark side, but there is no need to vilify them. Our WIMPs are a part of us that serves an important function. When we remember that they're designed to protect us, we can respond with kindness rather than disdain. We can turn them into an asset, because they offer data about something important that needs our attention. The WIMP wants to be seen, heard, and appreciated just like you, because it *is* you.

The transformative moment in leadership comes when we recognize the role our WIMPs play: trying and failing to offer us a cheap sense of safety that no longer serves us. By acknowledging and integrating the human aspects of vulnerability, uncertainty, and imperfection, leaders can turn what was once their kryptonite into their strongest asset.

This paradigm shift involves redefining strength not as the absence of vulnerability but as the courage to face it head on. Giving up on the illusion of superhuman prowess allows leaders to step into the power of being profoundly human. In doing so, leaders not only liberate themselves from the unrealistic expectations set by their WIMPs but also foster a more authentic, empathetic, and resilient leadership style throughout their organizations.

Self-compassion helps us see that we are not alone and that we share these insecurities and fears of rejection with almost every other human on earth. This feeling of shared humanity in self-compassion can curb the shame that often keeps us from seeking help, asking for what we need, and setting healthy boundaries. Self-compassion permits us to gently redirect our WIMPs and instead tell ourselves that we are allowed to feel bad and to focus on our physical, emotional, and mental needs and that we deserve to surround ourselves with supportive people. Accepting difficult feelings without trying to push them away actually lessens their impact and frequency and helps create psychological safety at work so everyone can more fully express themselves. Leaders, however, must pave the way.

Self-compassionate leadership transcends the quest for superhuman perfection by embracing the full spectrum of the human experience, including the well-intentioned, yet misinformed, protective instincts of our WIMPs. We finally recognize that our greatest strength is not invulnerability but our shared humanity and the courage to be authentically ourselves.

Another way to learn how to appreciate our WIMPs for their service is to understand the Internal Family Systems Model, which is an integrative approach to individual psychotherapy developed by Richard C. Schwartz in the 1980s.[9] It combines systems thinking with the view that the mind is made up of relatively discrete subpersonalities, each with its own unique viewpoint and qualities. Everyone has a Self to lead the individual's internal system, and each subpersonality has the potential to contribute positively to the Self, unless carried to extremes. Similarly, each WIMP has a beneficial side—a core strength that serves us well in moderation—which is often the reason why adopting this persona has led to success. It becomes a problem only when one of the WIMPs turns extreme or takes over completely.

If we're unaware of these parts of ourselves, and the way our fears manifest themselves as one or several WIMPs, we may slide toward an extreme where the negatives of a WIMP far outweigh the positives.

WOO-WOO WIN 》 Simon

Simon, one of my coaching clients in his early fifties, is a successful public relations executive for a global entertainment brand based in Los Angeles. He took great pride in his career and his ability to connect the brand to some of the world's biggest celebrities. His ambition, excellence, and drive for absolute control made his campaigns successful. However, when he moved into a more strategic role, away from the day-to-day operations, he struggled to delegate, give up control, and trust his team to execute his strategies. There was no room to fail and grow. He expected nothing less than perfection. The company suffered significant turnover among employees who were burnt out by the stress of Simon's leadership style.

Simon showed traits of multiple WIMPs, especially the perfectionist, but also the imposter and the people pleaser. As a perfectionist, he required everything his team produced to be flawless. Instead of leading, teaching, providing actionable feedback, and holding his team accountable, he micromanaged them, which only eroded their confidence. Simon felt like an imposter, doubting whether he could lead his team to do the work rather than doing the work himself. Because he was afraid leadership would find out he wasn't fit to set the direction and align his team to deliver on expectations, he was afraid to challenge last-minute, unreasonable requests. By trying to please leadership, he often failed to protect his team.

I took Simon through Kegan and Lahey's Immunity to Change Process, to explore unconscious resistance to changing their behavior no matter how much they try on the surface.[10] Simon uncovered his foundational assumption that if he and his team weren't perfect, they were worthless. He aspired to perfection because he believed it meant safety from having his team's impeccable reputation tarnished. His intent was to protect his team and his company. The results, however, were mistrust, anxiety, and drastically reduced performance.

He committed to facing the fear of being flawed, looking stupid or ill prepared, and even making significant mistakes in the service of creating space for growth and learning. He began to ask for help and feedback from his team and then used it to take action. He became dedicated to following up to ensure his team members felt heard. While acknowledging that perfectionism had served him to a point, he started to see that it also created unnecessary stress for him and others. Because he gave his team more autonomy while also extending trust, they felt more comfortable coming to him before big mistakes happened. By letting go of the assumption that he had to be perfect and by accepting a moderate risk of mistakes, he created an atmosphere of progress that empowered his team to do their best work.

WHO TRULY BRINGS THEIR "WHOLE SELF" TO WORK?

As kids, most of us experienced the desire to fit in and not stand out. Anything that made us different could become a cause for rejection, abandonment, or even bullying and violence. I spent my childhood years thinking I was stupid. A vague feeling of uncertainty followed me everywhere. I was out of step with everyone else, always behind, and seemingly unable to catch up. Being different often made me feel "less than" or "not good enough." I made up for it by being the class clown. I overcompensated by turning up the volume, being gregarious, and getting into trouble. I spent lots of time in the principal's office for doing dumb stuff. At times, I came off as apathetic about school. The truth is I cared so much about what others thought of me that I found it extremely painful when I couldn't figure out how to fit in. I was labeled a troublemaker, when I was just trying to survive in an environment where I struggled to thrive.

As adults, we can learn to embrace our differences and celebrate what makes us unique. In fact, we're encouraged to consider our differences a competitive advantage or unique value proposition. However, that programming from long ago is still in our coding, and we can fall back into the grown-up version of hiding and protecting ourselves. These self-protecting behaviors are a massive waste of time and energy and prevent us from truly testing the limits of what is possible.

Yet authenticity is a double-edged sword. We want to be authentic in organizations, but we don't want to show our weaknesses, uncertainty, fears, and limitations. To say we want to bring our authentic selves to work means not just wearing the clothes we like, showing our tattoos, or speaking freely. It requires us to accept our doubts and disappointments and to be honest without oversharing, so we can get as close to the truth as possible instead of becoming unreliable narrators of our own lives.

DON'T JUDGE YOURSELF FOR JUDGING YOURSELF

Most people, especially high-achieving individuals in leadership roles, are prone to believing their WIMPs' constant judgments. And it makes sense. The reasons you are a successful high achiever are varied, but one of them might very well be that you're overcompensating for the erroneous beliefs your WIMP subscribes to, always trying to prove yourself. Maybe you've got a chip on your shoulder. Perhaps you're still trying to convince your second-grade teacher, first boss, parent, or ex-spouse of your worth and value.

In her book *Trusting the Gold,* psychologist and meditation teacher Tara Brach explains that when emotions are strong, it's important to recognize they belong to us, but they are not us. I have an emotion, but I'm not the emotion itself.[11] There's nothing wrong with the rising anxiety, irritability, or aggression. They are our limbic caretakers, our survival brain's primitive way of trying to protect us and promote our well-being. Even self-judgment can be well intended because it tries to improve us to ensure our acceptance by loved ones, families, or communities.

Self-compassion can feel like an uphill battle because it goes against our biological wiring. An essential part of practicing self-compassionate leadership is reckoning with how much of our brain development, evolutionary conditioning, and biological urges may have been indispensable for physical survival in the distant past but is less useful for thriving in the modern world.

Humans lived in tribes for 150,000 years of our existence; we have learned there is security and survival in the tribe, in belonging to a family or group.[12] Banding together to compete for resources and engage in warfare with outsiders was an effective survival mechanism, but it was also the best way to meet our other needs—for belonging, family, and social interaction. Any action that threatens isolation or expulsion from the tribe is automatically considered risky. That's one reason we avoid seeking need fulfillment outside of our family or peer groups, even if it's much more likely that that's where we'd find it.

Our biological drive for survival and belonging to a tribe can override self-compassion, which requires conscious effort and can threaten evolutionary need fulfillment. As Yuval

Harari explains in his revelatory book *Sapiens*, evolution selected for tribalism because people who were more predisposed to adapting to a group and getting along within its hierarchy were more likely to survive and pass down their genes to the next generation.[13] It takes a tribe to raise a human, and evolution therefore favors those capable of forming strong social ties. Since humans are born underdeveloped, they are especially dependent on the care and protection of others and are open to being educated and socialized to a far greater extent than any other animal.

Even though I wasn't in any real danger at school, not fitting in felt like an existential threat. Similarly, even if being passed over for a promotion is not a life-or-death situation, it can feel like not only a threat to our livelihood but also a fundamental rejection of who we are.

WHY WE DEFAULT TO SUPPRESSING SELF-COMPASSION

Rejecting self-compassion as a human and as a leader comes naturally for most of us. Practicing self-compassion is incredibly difficult and requires concerted effort and strength. The false stories I believed about myself started in childhood and followed me into adulthood: *I'm not good enough. I'm stupid. I'm weak. I have to prove myself. I'm a fraud.* By now, you may be getting an idea about the false narratives you have replayed over and over in your own head. And as if mercilessly judging ourselves wasn't enough, we have tried to "fix" our supposed defects with perfectionism, self-criticism, or punishments.

Don't be surprised if this process feels awkward and scary at first. Challenging these old stories with self-compassion can feel counterintuitive, but it's the essential foundation for reaching our leadership potential. Although it's difficult, even painful, to dig into these hard truths about ourselves, it's also hard to continue on with our two jobs, listen to our WIMPs instead of our highest self, and always feel the need to hide and cover. Performing and pretending is hard. Being fully human as a self-compassionate leader is hard too. Often we don't have a choice between hard and easy. We only get to choose between two hard options. So pick your hard.

The next chapter will dig into my definition of self-compassionate leadership: its three integral aspects, what it is and isn't, and how to spot the traits of self-compassionate leadership in yourself and others.

2 » ZERO-FLUFF ZONE

What Is Self-Compassionate Leadership?

You don't want to beat yourself up for beating
yourself up in the vain hope that it will somehow
make you stop beating yourself up.

KRISTIN NEFF, *Self-Compassion*

Early in Sam Ramji's career, he climbed the ranks at one of
the biggest global software corporations until, as a senior director, he was offered a position as general manager. As part
of this new offer, he received a 360 assessment—are you sens-
ing a trend here? Sam received the same comprehensive feedback about his performance and areas of needed improvement that deeply affected Dan Harris and me.

While some of the feedback was positive, Sam also learned
that his team members thought he held others to a higher standard than himself. He relentlessly pushed for excellence on
his team but often fell short with his own performance. After
receiving the feedback, Sam decided not to take the general

manager role. He moved back to his home state, partly for personal reasons and partly to get the time and space to process the feedback and identify for himself where he needed to develop and grow.

One could view his decision as running away from a challenge or atoning for the negative feedback. Often, self-compassionate leadership doesn't look logical or successful from the outside. Sam took the feedback seriously and adopted a new role as an individual contributor for the next five years, shutting out the noise of being in a leadership position and responsible for a large team. He pushed himself as a developer to see if he could perform at the level of excellence he had expected from others.

Years later, he returned to executive leadership for a nonprofit because he believed the revenue burden of a corporation would have pushed him back toward being the type of leader he no longer wanted to be. Today, Sam is the cofounder and CEO of Sailplane, a public benefit corporation with a mission to elevate the future of human work, where artificial intelligence supports human intelligence.

Sam's path toward self-compassionate leadership resonated with me. I too spent years being miserable trying out traditional leadership approaches and received harsh feedback from the 360 assessment. Early in my career, I compensated for the not-good-enough feeling by buying into outdated leadership philosophies: *Watch your back. Don't trust anyone. Never let them see your weakness.* Like Will Ferrell's character Ricky Bobby in the movie *Talladega Nights,* I believed "if you're not first, you're last." This fundamentally false notion promotes constant social comparison and senseless competition. I tried to project confidence and smarts at all times while internally struggling with self-doubt and a sense of helplessness. My well-intentioned, misinformed protector (WIMP) showed up as an imposter and made me feel like a misfit, like the proverbial square peg trying to fit itself into a round hole.

Worse, all the external accolades, degrees, promotions, and career successes my achiever WIMP sought out never changed my internal chatter. I still didn't feel good enough, satisfied, or accomplished. I was blind to how this lack of self-worth impacted my behavior and coping mechanisms. I wasn't aware of the walls I had built and the armor I wore to compensate for, hide, and protect my insecurities. Even though I put myself out there, had a thriving social life, made good friends, and was generally well liked, I didn't like myself—not really.

WHAT EXACTLY IS SELF-COMPASSIONATE LEADERSHIP?

Self-compassionate leadership starts with acknowledging that we're human first. It is fundamentally defined by the title of the book: *Human First, Leader Second*.

Self-compassionate leadership comprises awareness, acceptance, and accountability—specifically, nonjudgmental awareness of our internal states, empathetic acceptance of our imperfect humanity, and thoughtful accountability for leading ourselves and others. I think of these three components as three domains for learning self-compassion. Along these lines, Bloom's Taxonomy is a framework for categorizing educational goals, objectives, and learning processes. First developed by Benjamin Bloom and colleagues in 1956, it has since undergone several revisions.[14] Bloom's Taxonomy divides learning into three domains: affective (heart), cognitive (head), and behavioral (hands). Bloom's concept can be applied to the three equally important aspects of the practice of self-compassion:

» Awareness happens in the affective domain, the heart, where we're aware of our experiences, thoughts, and feelings.

» Acceptance happens in our minds as we cognitively recognize our reality, accepting what is in and out of our control.

» Accountability allows us to take action into our own hands and behave with kindness toward ourselves.

These domains aren't mutually exclusive. Rather, they overlap and intersect to form the comprehensive practice that underlies the self-compassionate leadership model I will introduce in the next chapter.

THREE COMPONENTS OF SELF-COMPASSIONATE LEADERSHIP: AWARENESS, ACCEPTANCE, AND ACCOUNTABILITY

The three interconnected components of self-compassionate leadership are simple yet incredibly challenging practices—not because they impose a high cost of entry or demand an impressive pedigree or résumé. Awareness, acceptance, and accountability are challenging because they require courage, vulnerability, persistence, and the willingness to love yourself. The idea of loving oneself often connotes weakness, neediness, self-absorption, corniness, softness, or a kind of woo-woo mysticism. I assure you that the kind of self-love and self-compassion in this book is none of these. It will require you to experience great discomfort as you challenge your biases, beliefs, and assumptions. You will need to face your biggest demons without trying to destroy them but instead love them. This is all internal work that we must do within ourselves.

Awareness

Self-compassionate leaders have a deep understanding of their emotions, strengths, weaknesses, and triggers. They're aware of their inner experiences, feelings, and thoughts, which they note without judgment or self-criticism. When we direct this practice toward others, we call it empathy. By being self-aware, leaders recognize their limitations and areas for growth, enabling them to make more balanced and informed decisions. They are cognizant of their humanity.

Unfortunately, self-awareness has become a buzz word in organizations. Those who openly share how self-aware they are typically have blind spots, regardless of their best intentions. Saying you're self-aware doesn't make it so. You may truly be self-aware, but it's not because you tell someone you are. Awareness, like beauty, is, at least partially, in the eye of the beholder. Do others experience you as self-aware?

Awareness shifts with time and therefore is always shifting in and out of our focus. Our goal is to practice the skill of focusing in on what is here and now. Still, self-awareness is really hard. It requires us to be constantly curious about what we're experiencing—our feelings, thoughts, and triggers—and why. It means holding ourselves with both compassion and accountability to learn from this curiosity. What leaders often get wrong about self-awareness is that it requires us to know our strengths *and* weaknesses, our likes *and* dislikes, our light *and* dark sides.

Sometimes we think we can turn everything into a strength. If we just try hard enough, we mold ourselves into the kind of person who checks off all the right boxes (whatever we think they are). That's the opposite of being a self-compassionate leader. The point is to accept that we have both strengths and limitations. It's your choice what level of sacrifice in time and energy you want to make in pursuit of overcoming your limitations. Often, it's better to accept what is than fight against yourself and try to change something you're not fully committed to overcoming.

I'm a terrible typist who hates computer keyboards with a passion, although my handwriting is horrendous too. I use a computer every day, but I accept I'll never type at record speed. I'm not going to take a class to get better at this. It's not worth it to me, because I get by well enough, and I accept my slight frustrations. I'd love to ride a motorcycle up California's Pacific Coast Highway, but I'm too scared to actually do it. I'd love to learn a new language, but I can't be bothered with the time commitment. I'd like to be the kind of guy who loves going out to hear live music. But who I actually am is the kind of guy who doesn't enjoy standing around and getting bumped by strangers while it's way too loud to have a conversation.

Aside from the quirky preferences we all have, some of my deeper limitations include the tendency to become obsessive over small things. I've spent many late nights after work looking at thousands of light fixtures, tiles, and dining room chairs for our home remodel. Rationally, I know these details don't matter that much and that I'm driving my wife, Brie, mad with this strange preoccupation. I've started way too many fights over the perfect window trim. While it sounds like an argument out of a nineties sitcom, it really comes down to my extreme need for control, which can negatively impact my relationships with the people closest to me. Motorcycles and live music don't matter enough to me to cause me to put in the energy to change my personality or preferences. But letting go of my incessant need for control and obsession over irrelevant details is definitely important enough to lead me to make every effort.

What are those things you *want* to want but really don't? Is it the best use of your time to try and overcome your limitations rather than doubling down on your strengths? Maybe. Maybe not. Self-awareness helps you decide on a case-by-case basis. This, of course, also translates to your leadership personality, performance, and work style. Understanding yourself is the first important step, but it's crucial to discern between what calls for acceptance and what requires change.

The DISC assessment is a common psychometric tool used in organizations to understand different working styles. The results indicate which of the four main working styles you prefer:

D—dominance: drivers with a desire to get shit done

I—influence: collaborators who thrive on discussion, ideation, and socializing

S—steadiness: maintainers of the status quo who seek harmony

C—conscientiousness: analyzers of data who value precision in decision-making

I can't tell you how many times I have seen leaders un-knowingly (at least I'd like to think they are acting unknow-ingly) weaponize these concepts. "I'm a high D, so I'm just going to skip the niceties and get right down to the hard truth" or "I'm a high I, so forgive me if I grandstand or talk over you during this meeting." That's not self-awareness! To be truly self-aware, you must consider not only what you know about yourself but also how this impacts the people around you.

The first skill for self-awareness is "naming"—the ability to identify what's going on for you. For a high D, self-awareness could look like this: *I recognize my desire to skip the small talk and get down to business, but I also know that my team has put in a ton of work, so I will slow down and start by offering appreciation and checking in on how they are feeling.* A high I may catch themselves before jumping on a soapbox and in-stead ask a powerful question to hear the best thoughts from others before they share. As Tasha Eurich eloquently explains in her book *Insight*, self-awareness has two parts: what we know about ourselves and what we know about how other people perceive and experience us.[15]

Acceptance

Self-compassionate leaders acknowledge their imperfections and mistakes without harsh self-judgment. Instead of dwelling on failures, they treat themselves with kindness and under-standing, recognizing that making errors is an inherent part of growth and development. This self-acceptance allows them to learn from their experiences and demonstrate authenticity in their leadership. They accept themselves as a work in prog-ress in the context of their limitations and humanity.

Self-acceptance is all too often associated with weakness, apathy, and victimhood. This couldn't be further from the truth. When you're lost, it's not because you don't know where you want to go. It's because you don't know where you are. Self-acceptance means facing the reality of where you are so you know how to move ahead. Self-acceptance is the bedrock of personal accountability.

The skill of self-acceptance is rooted in our ability to normalize our hardest feelings—our shame, guilt, distrust, regret, disappointment, frustration, self-criticism, and unworthiness. Self-awareness first helps us identify what we are experiencing so we can name our feelings, which leads to connecting our personal experience to the shared experiences we all have as humans. This feeling of connectedness can foster self-acceptance, because we see ourselves as part of a whole.

One executive I worked with was confident that he would be selected when the COO position opened in his organization. Not only was he not asked to interview, but he was also blindsided when he found out that a replacement had already been hired. After spending 25 years of his career at the organization, he was devastated and began to question his loyalty to the company. He lost confidence in his value to the organization. When I asked him how a friend might feel in the same situation, he guessed they'd feel similar. When I asked what he'd say to this friend, he articulated what his friend needed to hear—what he himself needed to hear: "It makes sense you're disappointed after all the time you've dedicated to your company. It's frustrating to be blindsided like this and left wondering how this could have happened. Are you curious about other opportunities within the organization that might be a better fit? Can looking outside this company help you get clarity on where you truly want to be? Do you have trusted peers or mentors who can help you talk through your options? What questions do you need to ask to gain clarity?"

By naming and accepting his feelings of frustration, disappointment, betrayal, and anger, he did not become these emotions. He normalized them. He experienced the situation as most of us would, which didn't make him weak or wrong—simply human. By accepting the facts of the situation, he was able to offer feedback to his leadership, ask for clarity on what this meant for his future in the organization, and disprove much of the catastrophic scenario planning in his head. Shortly after, he was promoted to a position that better fit his skill set and now feels grateful for the leadership and broad experience of the new COO.

Accountability

Self-compassionate leaders prioritize their well-being and mental health. They understand that taking care of themselves is crucial for maintaining resilience, creativity, and productivity. This practice requires personal accountability and includes setting healthy boundaries, managing stress effectively, and seeking support when needed. By attending to their own needs, they can better support the well-being of their team members and foster a positive work environment.

Practicing accountability for self-kindness requires us to identify our needs and proactively work to address them. When we name and normalize a strong negative emotion, it can be a signpost to a fundamental unmet need. In some cases, self-kindness can be about asking for help when the workload is too much or the priorities are unclear. In other cases it can mean holding ourselves accountable for not stepping up to support our team when they need recognition and inspiration.

Self-compassionate leaders discern whether to move leeward or windward in any given situation and take accountability either way. You may have heard Rory Vaden's popular story about the diametrically opposed behavior of cattle and buffalo in a snowstorm.[16] When a snowstorm sweeps across the Great Plains, cattle will stand still waiting for the storm to pass. In contrast, buffalo will run directly into the gale in an attempt to come out the other side more quickly. While the cattle remain unmovable and engulfed in the storm, the buffalo seek it out and face it head on.

Outdated leadership philosophies might highlight the buffalo's behavior as the sort of go-getter attitude characteristic of effective leaders, whereas the cattle might be considered passive and indecisive. However, we can also see the buffalo as impatient, impulsive, and too quick to take major risks, whereas the cattle have the stamina, strength, and equanimity to ride out the storm.

Sometimes you'll need the buffalo's boldness, sometimes the cattle's composure. You'll know if you must square your shoulders and run straight into the chaos or if you need to be unflappable and steady while the storm rages around you. Both buffalo and cattle will get through the storm. Both approaches can present an opportunity for growth, self-discovery, and trust building with your team. Ultimately, you'll be accountable for whichever approach you choose.

HOW TO USE THE THREE As OF SELF-COMPASSIONATE LEADERSHIP

It's helpful to remember awareness, acceptance, and account-ability as the three aspects of self-compassionate leadership that we can apply to whatever situation we're facing person-ally or professionally. Here is an example of how to use them in practice:

Awareness: I feel...

Example: I feel exhausted and frustrated, because I've been working late all week, trying to finish the board presentation by myself.

Acceptance: I am...

Example: I am under a lot of pressure and want to make sure this presentation goes well. I'm also human and in need of sleep. It makes sense that I'm tired. I'm a member of this team, and being frustrated at others not carrying their weight is normal. I am prone to take over projects so it's possible part of this frustration is self-inflicted.

Accountability: I will...

Example: I will ask my team members for help. I will step back, delegate tasks, and avoid micromanaging everyone's contributions. I will let go of the illusion that the presentation will be perfect, or even just better, if I do it on my own. I will learn from this mistake and do it differently next time.

WHAT SELF-COMPASSIONATE LEADERSHIP IS NOT

I shared my concept of self-compassionate leadership first, including the three As—awareness, acceptance, and accountability—so it's fresh in your mind when we now dive into the discussion of what self-compassionate leadership is *not*.

Self-Compassion Is Not an Excuse for Bad Behavior and Unhealthy Coping Mechanisms

Self-compassion can mean relaxing through a couple of episodes of your favorite show when you've had a stressful week at work, but it keeps you from going on a weekend-long reality TV binge to avoid addressing a problem. If you're dealing with a hard situation at work, self-compassion teaches you to sit with the anger, frustration, fear, and sadness and then allows the anger to activate your problem-solving skills and courage to change.

In my coaching practice, I model self-compassion to my clients in the same way. If a client comes in frustrated and ready to vent, I listen intently, but I also make sure I set a time limit. For ten minutes, you can get everything that's upsetting you off your chest, and I will be 100 percent present and empathetic. Once that time is up, we'll step into coaching and discuss what you will do about this situation. *What's going on for you? What's the story you're telling yourself? What assumptions are you making? What outcome do you want? What are the next best steps to take?* This is an example of being supportive and kind by being invested in my client's best interest, as I model how to walk that line.

You may think that you can get through that complex project at work without extending self-compassion but may overlook the fact that you instead gravitate toward comfortable yet unhealthy coping mechanisms. Author Phoebe Long explains what helps her avoid falling into these traps: "In moments of difficulty, I plan to take a self-compassion break. If I'm tempted to drink during the week, I might cultivate self-kindness by placing a hand on my heart and saying, 'May I be healthy' or 'May I act wisely'; mindfulness by saying, 'I'm having an urge to drink' or 'I'm feeling stressed'; and common humanity by saying, 'This is what it's like to struggle with a goal' or 'Other people have felt this way, too.'"[17]

It can feel awkward to use self-compassion by physically soothing yourself, such as by placing a hand on your heart, holding yourself in a tight hug, or massaging your temples. You may think it's cringy and strange, but is it really worse than taking the edge off every night with a drink or maxing out your credit cards to buy another thing you don't need off an Instagram ad?

Self-Compassion Is Not the Same As Toxic Positivity

Toxic positivity is more extreme than a glass-half-full mentality. Toxic positivity prevents us from dealing with difficult work situations, team dynamics, or project setbacks. It's a lazy shortcut used to gloss over problems that require self-reflection and may cause us pain or discomfort but that also hold insights and treasures that could help us progress and evolve. Toxic positivity is *The Lego Movie*'s title song, "Everything Is Awesome," or the Instagram platitudes admonishing "good vibes only." Personally, I'm here for whatever is honest and real, silly laugh or ugly cry.

The core of toxic positivity is denying, minimizing, and invalidating the fullness of the human experience, over-indexing on the silver lining of everything, and focusing exclusively on the good in a situation. Toxic positivity takes us to an artificially cheery place, like the cartoonish facade of Disneyland. But businesses are run in reality, not la-la land, and problems aren't solved by pretending they don't exist.

Self-compassion is the antidote to toxic positivity. If you're in a leadership position, self-compassion that invites compassion for others is immensely helpful in coaching a team member or employee through a difficult situation. You will be better equipped to listen and understand before rushing into solutions born of the discomfort of challenging feelings and situations.

The first step as a leader is to help your team member identify and label the feeling without judgment. You will earn your team member's trust by validating their feelings without getting stuck in a passive misery loop. Empathy and validation can go a long way toward helping someone move through a difficult emotion or situation, because they're no longer alone in it. No coaching, change, or problem solving can happen before the reality as experienced by the person has been acknowledged. Only after that first step is completed can you start coaching your employee and encouraging them to proactively assess the situation, build resilience in the face of difficulties, and devise next steps.

Self-Compassion Is Not a Different Word for Self-Esteem

A group of bright and talented University of California, Berkeley, students were divided into three subgroups and took the same difficult exam that was designed to fail all the students. Following the test, each of the three groups received a different message. The first group received one of self-compassion: "If you had difficulty with this test, you're not alone. It's common for students to have difficulty with tests like this." The second group was given a message that focused on their self-esteem: "You must be intelligent if you got into Berkeley!" The third group acted as the control group and was given no message after the test.[18]

The researchers assumed that students at a highly competitive university would judge themselves harshly for failing a test, and they wanted to understand whether different messaging would have an effect on the students, who were all allowed to study for as long as they wanted before taking the exam a second time. The group that received the self-compassionate message studied the longest, displayed the greatest motivation to improve following the initial failure, and scored highest on the second test. It appears that self-compassion (accepting our struggles and weaknesses) is more effective than self-esteem (focusing on our strengths) when facing a painful failure.

MOVING BEYOND GENDERED STEREOTYPES OF SELF-COMPASSIONATE LEADERSHIP

Besides misguided assumptions about self-compassionate leadership, I've also come across strong gender bias regarding this leadership approach. Research shows that skills often categorized as feminine yield higher economic returns. Women's proficiency in promoting vulnerability, compassion, and psychological safety is gaining recognition.[19] CEOs are noting the impact of these skills on the bottom line, and studies are drawing connections between business performance and character strengths like compassion.[20]

Conversely, research indicates a troubling trend for boys and men, who are experiencing fewer friendships, less socialization, and a reluctance to seek help. The societal pressure to conform to traditional masculine norms often discourages men from expressing emotions, contributing to a cycle of isolation, unaddressed mental health issues, and adverse health outcomes.[21] Men's reluctance to seek help for mental health issues, often stemming from societal perceptions of masculinity, can have fatal consequences. Men are notably more likely than women to die by suicide, making it clear that the constraints of gender norms are not a "female problem" or a "male problem"—they're a human problem. Suicide rates are alarmingly high, particularly among white males aged 45–49, illustrating the urgency of addressing these issues.[22]

Self-compassion can serve as a crucial alleviator of these worrisome trends, and women may have a head start in this area. Men and women embark from different starting points in nearly every aspect of life. Women might find an early footing through their social circles, where discussing emotions is embraced. They are guided by influential voices like Mel Robbins, Glennon Doyle, and Oprah Winfrey, who have championed compassion and empathy for years. Men, on the other hand, encounter messages from figures like Andrew Huberman, David Goggins, and Jocko Willink, who emphasize relentless optimization.

For men reading this, cultivating self-compassion might feel like uncharted territory, perhaps uncomfortable, because of entrenched cultural expectations around gender. Kindness and compassion toward oneself are qualities not traditionally celebrated in men. Yet the objective remains: fostering self-compassion skills enriches our lived experiences. This book may push you beyond your comfort zone, and I invite you to do so with compassion, knowing that you're not alone in your challenges, stressors, and fears.

Of course, our varied struggles with self-compassion and its application to leadership are not based on societal expectations regarding sex and gender alone. How much access we have to people modeling self-compassion depends on our family, culture, and religion. What we're taught about whether we "deserve" love and kindness often depends on cultural biases regarding race, able-bodiedness, or sexual orientation. In short, many intertwined threads impact how much or how little access we've had to self-compassion as individuals and members of our various communities.

Every single one of us deserves and needs self-compassion. We all inhabit different starting points, but self-compassionate leadership is possible and accessible for all of us.

EXERCISE » Moment of Truth

Consider this your starting point—the red arrow on the map that shows "you are here." There's no judgment regarding how many of these statements you hold to be true for yourself. It's only a quick thought exercise to give you a sense of where you are right now.

You might be a self-compassionate leader if one or more of the following statements applies to you:

» You have strong opinions loosely held.

» You know the final outcome is not a reflection of your value. Your value is as much about *how* you contribute as *what* you contribute.

» You are aware of your emotions and respond to them with objectivity and curiosity. You don't say "I'm angry," but "I'm feeling angry because I was not included in an important decision that will impact my team."

» You remember in the hard times that you're not alone or the only one who has struggled. Other people have had similar experiences.

» You are vulnerable but do not overshare or overexpose.

» You are present but not needy. You're able to make others feel seen, heard, and appreciated without constantly needing the same in return.

» You are prepared for things to go badly but don't expect that they will.

» You take your work seriously but not yourself.

» You can make a mistake and quickly recover to mine the lessons for growth.

» You can receive difficult feedback while both managing the hurt or discomfort and receiving the message as positively intended.

» You can engage in a difficult conversation without taking responsibility for the other person's emotional response.

» When your emotions are triggered by someone's behavior, you use personal accountability to understand what triggered you and why.

Exercising self-compassion can seem like we're cutting ourselves too much slack or failing to accept responsibility, and as leaders we often resist it. Self-criticism and judgment are considered tough and honest, while self-compassion is seen as weak and fluffy. It's important to remember, however, that practicing self-compassion won't make us quit but, as demonstrated in the Berkeley experiment, actually motivates us to try harder and improve ourselves in the long term. This is just as true when applied to our leadership approach.

Now that you understand what self-compassionate leadership is and isn't and have reflected on your familial, social, and cultural conditioning, I'll introduce you to the Ward Model—my framework for applying theory to practice.

3 » THE WARD MODEL

Navigating the Roundabout of Self-Compassionate Leadership

> A moment of self-compassion can change your entire day. A string of such moments can change the course of your life.
>
> CHRISTOPHER K. GERMER,
> *The Mindful Path to Self-Compassion*

In the early twentieth century, the Monte Carlo Casino in Monaco was famous not only for its luxurious gambling halls but also for a peculiar and somewhat grim pastime for the wealthy elite: pigeon shooting. The casino raised pigeons on a nearby rooftop and would hold the birds in a tunnel beneath the casino to be released at regular intervals. The birds, unaware of their fate, would fly out of the tunnel where the casino patrons waited, armed with shotguns.

The birds who survived the first round would head home to the rooftop, only to be returned to the tunnel again and again until every last one got picked off. Imagine a scenario where a surviving pigeon didn't go back home for another round of old-school first-person shooter games but instead chose a different path. This decision would represent a profound shift in the pigeon's behavior, symbolizing the awakening of self-awareness and the questioning of ingrained patterns. Of course, this wouldn't happen. We're talking about birds with bird brains here.

A pigeon can't break the cycle of predictability that continuously leads it to danger and, eventually, death. But humans can—at least theoretically. It's the execution of the concept that's a little elusive. We might be quick to judge the pigeons, but our much more evolved brains frequently embody this quote attributed to Albert Einstein: "Insanity is doing the same thing over and over and expecting different results." One way to teach ourselves to interrupt these automatic reactions, default thought patterns, and repetitive behaviors is the Ward Model I've created.

WHAT IS THE WARD MODEL?

The Ward Model is a self-compassionate leadership framework I've developed to help you get to know your well-intentioned, misinformed protectors (WIMPs), quit your second job of "covering," and break free from the cycles of emotions, thoughts, and behaviors that keep you stuck, burn you out, and prevent you from living a life aligned with your core values and vision. The Ward Model allows you to become aware of what's happening inside and around you at any given moment, accept your complex humanity without judgment, and be accountable for the next intentional step you take and, ultimately, for how you show up in your life.

The suffix "-ward" is usually attached to the word indicating a particular spatial or temporal direction, such as "forward" (to the front) or "backward" (to the back). I call the framework the Ward Model as a reminder of the six main directions or paths we can take to become self-compassionate leaders.

The Six Directions within the Ward Model

I view the six directions of the Ward Model as entry points or on-ramps to self-compassionate leadership. Imagine a traffic roundabout with six roads leading into the center from all directions. They're all equally capable of serving as an entry point to the inner circle of self-compassion.

» Inward: focusing on internal physical, emotional, and mental states

» Outward: understanding our intent and impact on the external world

» Backward: reflecting on past experiences and learning from them

» Forward: recognizing future potential and aligning with aspirations

» Windward: facing challenges with forgiveness and accountability

» Leeward: seeking comfort, safety, rest, and recovery

I encourage you to experiment with all of the entry points, especially if you're more comfortable or familiar with certain directions over others. Each on-ramp leads to the same destination but offers unique discoveries on the way to a comprehensive understanding and practice of self-compassionate leadership.

While each path may begin as an affirming exercise to deliberately be kinder to yourself, it's just as valid to start from a place of self-criticism or self-protection. After all, that's where we need self-compassion the most. In other words, how you feel doesn't matter—every feeling, "good" or "bad," can become the access point for the Ward Model. When you're kicking ass and feeling on top of the world, use the Ward Model proactively to center yourself. When you find yourself stuck in a WIMP-driven defensive pattern, remember that that's just the shadow side of the same path or on-ramp. The Ward Model meets you where you're at, right now, in this moment.

The Three Dualities within the Ward Model

Each of the on-ramps or entry points has a natural opposite, so I find it helpful to think of the six directions as pairs that complement each other and teach us about the three aspects of self-compassionate leadership: awareness, acceptance, and accountability (figure 1).

The Dualities Inward and Outward Represent Awareness

We cultivate awareness by focusing both on our internal thoughts and feelings and on how we show up in interactions with others and our environments. These directions help us be aware and present so we can move toward congruence of our inward experience and outward expression.

Of course, we don't always need to possess full awareness to understand where we fall on the spectrum of inward and outward. It's precisely the times when we find ourselves internally ruminating, experiencing feelings about our feelings,

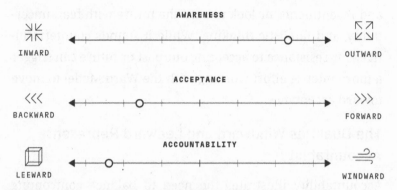

FIGURE 1. The Ward Model Duality Pairs. The pairs of dualities within the Ward Model correspond with awareness, acceptance, and accountability. We constantly move between the dualities; the circles indicate where we might fall at any one moment.

making up stories about other people's intentions, or externally reacting instead of responding that we need the Ward Model to dip into awareness. With time, we'll get better at spotting these incidents of being unaware of our internal states and external expressions so we can intentionally pause to apply the Ward Model to increase our awareness.

The Dualities Backward and Forward Represent Acceptance

Acceptance involves understanding our backstory and past experiences so we can leverage them to move toward our future potential. Acceptance comes from connecting with our own story and the stories of others through our common humanity.

This acceptance often comes after we first struggle with replaying old stories from the past, get stuck in fixed mindsets and resentments, or look toward the future with fear, uncertainty, and fatalistic thinking. While it sounds counterintuitive, our resistance to accepting our past or future can trigger a more intense effort working with the Ward Model to move toward acceptance.

The Dualities Windward and Leeward Represent Accountability

Accountability illustrates the need to balance confronting challenges head-on in the windward direction with seeking safety and rest to recharge in the leeward direction. We're accountable to ourselves for managing this symmetry of courage and comfort.

You can use the Ward Model even if you're noticing opposite behaviors of self-abandonment, avoidance, or numbing in the leeward direction along with stonewalling, defensiveness, or control in the windward direction. In fact, these shadow sides are prime examples of when working with the model will be most beneficial in helping you achieve full accountability.

The Ward Model illustrates and explores the tensions we all navigate between the six directions and three dualities, offering different entry points or on-ramps to our self-compassionate leadership practice. It wouldn't truly be a model for gaining greater self-compassion if it didn't help us specifically when we needed it the most, in our feelings of pity and indifference, when we are nearly shut down in self-protection. Whether we're aware or unaware, accepting or unaccepting, accountable or unaccountable, there are no prequalifications we must meet, preliminary work

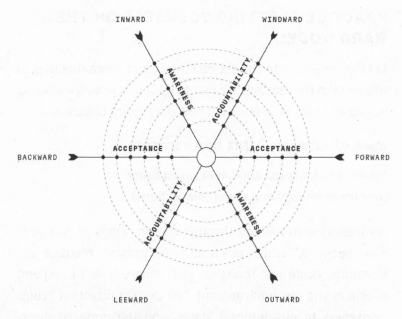

FIGURE 2. The Ward Model with Its Three Duality Pairs Made Up of Six On-Ramps. Where are you in this moment? Finding your particular position between each of the three dualities can help you see more clearly where you are along the on-ramps and where you have to compensate or calibrate.

we must complete, or conditions we must create to use the Ward Model as a start to move from self-abandonment to self-compassion.

Understanding each direction and duality pair separately and how these competing tensions interact with each other in our lives allows us to plot our current location within the Ward Model at any given time. You can start today, right now, exactly the way you are.

PRACTICE PLOTTING YOURSELF ON THE WARD MODEL

Let's go deeper into the six directions and three dualities to understand the tensions we all navigate and practice plotting ourselves within the model at any given point (figure 2).

Inward/Outward: Paths to Awareness

How to navigate the tension between being (our inner reality) and doing (our actions)

Awareness is developed through the on-ramps of "inward" and "outward," which teach us to be present, regulate our emotions, guide our thoughts, and choose how to respond to others and our environment. The inward direction brings awareness to our internal states, and the outward direction illuminates the intent and impact of our behaviors and interactions.

"Inward" is about recognizing your feelings and thoughts at any given moment. What insights do they provide about your physical, emotional, and mental needs? Meeting your own needs isn't the same as being needy. It's about acknowledging your human nature. The advice about putting on your own oxygen mask first is clichéd but true. Addressing your own needs makes you a better leader and allows you to focus on supporting your team.

Your "outward" interactions and behaviors reflect how your inner narratives, feelings, and beliefs manifest themselves externally. Say you just left a frustrating meeting with your manager and are reeling from the corrective feedback. *Why did I make such a stupid mistake? I should have known better.* This narrative of "I'm not good enough" carries into the next meeting, where your team needs your full attention and support. But now you're on edge and expect your team to operate without error to relieve your own feelings of inadequacy. No more mistakes can be made. Your mood sucks the energy right out of the room and leaves a lasting impact on your team. You can almost see the thought bubbles popping up above their heads: *Oh no, he's pissed. Don't ask too many questions. Just say yes and move on.* You're momentarily satisfied that they got the message, but you already feel your gut twisting with the knowledge that the leader you want to be is not who's standing in front of your team right now.

It's crucial to align your "inward" and "outward" experiences. When they're misaligned or poorly managed, you can become trapped within your own thoughts and feelings, detached from the reality of outside circumstances. Alternatively, you might get so caught up in the outer world that you become disconnected from the internal signals and signposts trying to alert you that you're moving in the wrong direction.

Are you a "human being" or a "human doing"? Most of us are preoccupied with what we "need to do" in order to be. *Need to get a good education to be successful. Need to act strong to be respected. Need to earn a lot of money to be happy.* We're taught from childhood to focus on doing, with most adults expecting us to grow out of our natural state of being. Instead of learning from kids, who are excellent at being present in the moment, we tell them to focus on the future and think about what they need to do to get there. Living in an action-oriented way instead of a feeling-oriented way becomes an automatic reaction for us over time.

It's crucial to balance both, especially in our culture, which often stresses *doing* at the expense of *being*. Our society prizes action. In emergency situations we often admonish each other or ourselves: "Don't just stand there, do something!" This focus on doing invites reactivity and impulsivity, because we don't allow ourselves a pause to check "inward" first. Self-compassion lets us prioritize accepting our physical sensations, bringing our thoughts in alignment with our values, and processing our emotions to calm and ground our being before we jump into doing.

Mindfulness is enormously helpful in navigating this tension and becoming aware of our current state. Mindfulness is not a fluffy, meditative practice as much as it is self-awareness paired with acceptance that leads to accountability. The practice of checking in with ourselves and observing our "inward" state is closely linked to accepting how these internal experiences impact our external actions. Our behaviors are reactions or responses to stimuli. A stimulus can be internal (hunger, a need to stretch, fatigue, or pain), or external (traffic, a rude comment from your boss, a boring meeting). Paying attention to how we internally process a stimulus can make the difference between an automatic reaction and a thoughtful response. Real mindfulness fosters presence and awareness that allow us to pause, check in, and reset before we move on to the next task, meeting, or project so we can respond rather than react.

Self-awareness is a precursor to the ability to respond, rather than react, because it allows us to process and evaluate information. Most leaders are so busy and overwhelmed that they default to habitual or fear-based reactions instead of taking the time to pause and survey a situation, allowing space for self-reflection and awareness. These leaders may think they don't have time to pause, but their reactivity can necessitate time-consuming repair of damaged relationships, land them in the HR office, and severely limit their careers.

Dean, one of my clients, came to me through a referral from his HR office. In his late forties, he was a former Drug Enforcement Administration agent turned supply chain executive. He was hardened by his past and the things he'd seen and experienced. He didn't want to be there and made sure I knew it. He was a typical old-school, hard-ass executive who believed in "brutal honesty" that bordered on cruelty. He liked to see himself as a servant leader, but HR complaints painted him as much more of a relentlessly critical dictator. His team ceased being innovative because everyone was scared to speak up with ideas for fear of ridicule. Though his inner circle experienced him as charming and gregarious and laughed at his jokes, even when they were cruel or inappropriate, his team perceived him as cold and detached. Using the on-ramp of "inward" was Dean's first step in becoming aware that his defensive and controlling leadership style was born out of his own self-judgment and terror about being picked apart for the smallest flaw. It offered an entry point for deploying the self-compassion that would guide him from awareness to acceptance and finally accountability.

The first step of awareness via the "inward" and "outward" on-ramps happens in the now. What sensations are you experiencing in your body right now? Hunger, fatigue, muscle tension? What are you thinking about? Which data points are you selecting from all the information available to you right now?

Are you focusing on your boss's seemingly annoyed facial expression, or do you give more weight to your team's favorable feedback on your presentation? Are you aware of the biases guiding your selectivity? How do you feel in this moment? Is your "not-good-enough" story creeping in and making you anxious and fidgety? Or are you so happy and satisfied with your team's response that you dismiss your boss's irritation?

Considering all the data available to you at any given moment can feel overwhelming, but you can also see it as a million chances to recalibrate and course correct at any moment. You don't have to keep going down that road if it looks like a dead end. You can turn around at any time and make a different choice. That's the power of mindful awareness in helping you navigate the tension between "inward" and "outward."

This awareness is the foundation for accepting your current state, whatever that may be.

Backward/Forward: Paths to Acceptance

How to navigate the tension between context (our past experiences) and clarity (our future vision)

You find acceptance by understanding and letting go of where you've been and where you want to go. The "backward" direction is an on-ramp that helps us acknowledge our history while the "forward" direction allows us to accept our values and align our goals and vision accordingly.

"Backward" is where you came from, your lived experience, and your backstory. It's where you grew up, your community, culture, and family. It's your relationships with parents and siblings and extended family, including all the old stories about yourself and the resulting limiting beliefs. Each of these informs the context that makes up your daily lived experience. Did you experience lack or abundance, stability or insecurity? How did your experience shape your worldview and impact your decisions? Your history informs who you are today and why, but it doesn't keep you from changing.

Although your backstory is unique, everyone you meet also has their own backstory. Each of our backstories gives context to how we arrived at this point. We don't have the same experiences, but we can see our common humanity in the fact that all of us are shaped by our pasts, struggling against the burdens of old coping mechanisms and working to accept the gifts. By understanding both our own context and that of others, we can identify commonalities and draw strength from shared experiences.

As leaders with diverse backgrounds, we all share a common thread: each of us has navigated the complexities and challenges of life and leadership, striving to do our best. Every leader, even heavyweights like Tim Cook (Apple), Sheryl Sandberg (Meta), or Satya Nadella (Microsoft), had to start somewhere, traveling the same path you're currently on. It's vital to recognize this shared experience, while accepting the unique aspects of our backstories. We're not alone in asking ourselves what parts of our histories might be holding us back—and, more important, what untapped potential could drive us forward. Our past is always informing our path into the future. Are you running away from something or toward something?

I believe if you extend "backward" and "forward" far enough, they will eventually meet, creating a circle. Salmon are born in freshwater rivers, spend most of their lives in the ocean, and then return to the place they were born to lay eggs. Once salmon end their journey and leave fertilized eggs in new reeds, they have completed their life cycle and die shortly after. The salmon carcasses then are distributed by the river's current along the watershed to provide nutrients to other species, while their young hatch and start the life cycle all over again. I have a large salmon tattoo on my right ribcage, reminding myself to honor where I came from, where I'm going, and where I will eventually return to.

"Forward" is about creating clarity on the vision for your future. What are your hopes and dreams? How do you measure success? How do you know whether your definition of success is genuinely your own or is influenced by your organization, background, or other people? I often work with leaders caught up in the thought "I'm not there yet." They're constantly seeking the next title or promotion while perpetually feeling inadequate. The dissatisfaction often stems from their lacking a clear understanding of their future vision, so they can't fully appreciate how far they've come and where they are right now. When I help these leaders gain a realistic perspective on their current situation and then define their future goals, it shifts their focus. Instead of fixating on the distant horizon and wondering when they'll arrive, they can concentrate on the present and on leading their teams effectively. They can trust themselves and their teams, confident in the direction they're headed.

Finding acceptance for our past and where we are right now, enables us to take accountability for what we need to do next to get where we want to go.

Leeward/Windward: Paths to Accountability

How to navigate the tension between comfort (our safety)
and courage (the unknown)

Accountability encompasses both the courage to face problems and the capacity to care for ourselves with kindness. When we take the "windward" on-ramp, we're holding ourselves accountable for facing a challenge, setting a difficult boundary, or crawling out from a rock-bottom moment. The "leeward" on-ramp helps us be accountable for our own well-being by taking responsibility for filling our needs for rest, recovery, comfort, and safety. If you're in danger of burnout, try the "leeward" on-ramp first!

"Leeward" refers to the side of a ship or island sheltered from the wind. In the Ward Model, it represents seeking safety, comfort, and tranquility. It's akin to finding a calm, protective space where one can rest, recover, and rejuvenate away from life's challenges and stressors. On a daily basis, it can look like taking a lunch break to go for a walk, not answering emails on vacation, or exercising before work. "Leeward" actions add to your well-being and are basic self-care practices regarding sleep and rest, nutrition and exercise, play and social connection.

Of course, the familiar choices we turn to for comfort aren't always the most beneficial ones. I know eating an entire bucket of ice cream and inhaling every last cookie in the house isn't the optimal course of action. And yet that's what I want to do instead of eating a real meal and doing a short meditation. "Leeward" can sometimes turn from safety to passivity, when we start avoiding pressing issues, distract ourselves from problems instead of facing them, or refuse to make improvements because "this is how we've always done it." Whether we're falling into our default comforts or choosing healthier practices, these elements for reestablishing safety and predictability typically fit within the realm of the known.

"Windward" refers to the side of a ship or island facing the wind. In the Ward Model, it symbolizes facing challenges head-on, much like a ship braving the storm. It's about confronting difficulties, overcoming obstacles, and demonstrating resilience and courage in the face of adversity. "Windward" represents the unexplored expanse characterized by courage in the face of uncertainty. This is where big dreams, audacious goals, leaps of faith, and risky bets collide with rock-bottom moments, disaster, and complete failure. It's stepping out of your comfort zone into the proverbial unknown. It's exciting and mysterious and full of potential, but if it doesn't work out, there's a hefty price to pay. In the best case, you will bravely move toward what you want. In the worst case, you may find yourself sliding toward recklessness.

I help my clients actively create these "windward" experiences, which may include speaking up in a meeting, declining a new project, or asking for a promotion. These actions might involve working with a coach like me to address personal and professional difficulties, seeing a therapist, ending an unhealthy relationship, forgiving yourself, or starting a new business. It's a matter of asking, *What if I did X, even though I'm scared?*

If you focus too much on self-comforting practices, your

"leeward" behaviors will have diminishing returns because you never challenge yourself. If you're focusing on "windward" actions exclusively, always heading straight into the darkest forest without proper provisions, maps, and guides, you'll eventually get lost. Dean's well-intentioned, misinformed protector (WIMP) tried both extreme approaches simultaneously to keep him safe from rejection (hard-ass) and humiliation (imposter). On the "windward" dimension, he felt intense guilt about how he treated his team and shame for not being a better leader in those rock-bottom and make-or-break moments. His "leeward" need for comfort resulted in detachment and isolation because he had no tools to take care of himself in a gentler, kinder way.

Navigating this tension between comfort and courage requires accountability and a commitment to treating yourself with care and understanding. Both "leeward" and "windward" actions can constitute self-kindness, and both can feel unsettling depending on which direction you skew by default. If you're more comfortable in the "windward" space, you may have a hard time taking care of yourself by going home early and nursing your cold. If you tend toward the "leeward" approach, it may be more difficult for you to work out a difficult problem on your own instead of prematurely asking for help from a team member.

Learning accountability through the on-ramps of "windward" and "leeward" takes practice. Whichever on-ramp we choose as our first entry point, it's highly likely that the process will make us much more aware of how and when one of our WIMPs will show up.

The Ward Model as the Antidote to Our WIMPs

Whenever our well-intentioned, misinformed protectors show up, we can remind ourselves that they're only trying to keep us safe. While they can bring out a whole range of thoughts, emotions, and behaviors that are decidedly not self-compassionate, they can also serve as the avatars of our shadow side, which often provide the most salient entry points or on-ramps to the Ward Model (figure 3). Their presence is an opportunity to ask how we can use self-compassion, instead of the extreme measures our WIMPs default to, in order to take care of ourselves. The unknown can scare us, and the known can bore us. There is immense value in balancing the dualities of doing and being, context and clarity, courage and comfort. Our WIMPs can guide us toward the dimension that most desperately needs our self-compassion practice.

Once I started working with Dean, the hard-ass executive you met earlier in the chapter, he opened up much more quickly than I expected. For three decades he'd had a contentious relationship with his father-in-law, who considered Dean unworthy of his daughter. Dean's father-in-law was powerful in the community and highly successful professionally. His opinion carried a lot of weight, so Dean had felt crushed under the burden of proving himself for thirty years.

Through our work together, Dean realized that he'd been hypocritical: he had considered himself a servant leader when he was as judgmental toward his team as his father-in-law was to him. He was perpetuating the exact behavior that had caused him the most anguish. The WIMPs show up to keep us alive when we feel threatened to the point where we fight,

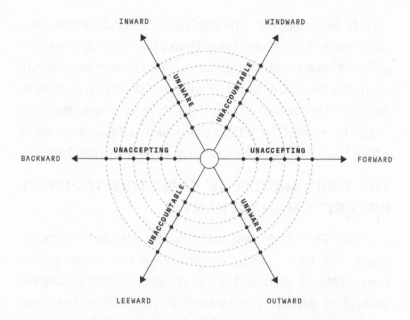

FIGURE 3. Using Your Shadow Side to Access the Ward Model.
If you find yourself in self-abandonment mode, battling your
WIMPs and feeling unaware, unaccepting, and unaccountable, ask
yourself: Where are you stuck right now? Where along the three
dualities do you want to start? Spoiler alert: There's no incorrect
answer. Every point can serve as an on-ramp to the center of
self-compassion.

flee, freeze, or fawn. In my work with Dean, I saw how his
perfectionist, hard-ass, imposter, and achiever WIMPs traded
off, depending on the situation. They tried to keep him safe
from his father-in-law's ridicule by causing him to judge himself even more harshly. His internal self-criticism, designed to
push him to peak performance, instead manifested itself in
outwardly controlling and domineering behavior.

Only by deploying self-compassion instead of merciless judgment toward himself was Dean able to process his own pain and take accountability for the pain he was causing others. Using the Ward Model to teach my clients about how to navigate the tensions between the three dualities, and how to gently redirect the WIMPs that will inevitably show up, is a new application of what is known as polarity management.

THE WARD MODEL: AN EFFECTIVE TOOL FOR POLARITY MANAGEMENT

Coaching Dean and many other diverse clients through the years, I've seen a recurring challenge that keeps people stuck—polarity management. Barry Johnson introduces the concept of polarity management in his book of the same name.[23] He explains that accepting the extremes helps us find equanimity and balance in the ebb and flow, by not skewing too heavily in one direction.

I created the Ward Model as a tool for illustrating the tensions we navigate between the three dualities, thereby allowing us to assess where we are on each spectrum at any given moment. The concept of polarity management helps us understand that we're always moving between opposing poles, between inward and outward, backward and forward, windward and leeward. Using the Ward Model, we first become aware of our position between the poles, then accept what got us here in the first place, and finally become accountable for moving toward balance in the center. Each of the six on-ramps is equally suited as an entry point, and I invite you to pick the one that fits best in any given moment. All roads lead not to Rome but to self-compassion in the center.

I worked with Dean on the "inward/outward" dimension, but that's just one way to slice the cake. Dean was also experiencing the tension of being pulled "backward" into his past while trying to move "forward" into his future. The repetition of old stories about his worthlessness perpetuated by his father-in-law kept him stuck. Focusing on projecting "outward" strength and competence was masking a deep "inward" need to feel valued and accepted. Eventually, this caused Dean to make reactive decisions to prove he could match his father-in-law's ambition and success (windward) at the expense of giving himself a break or cutting his team any slack (leeward). In other words, it doesn't matter which on-ramp you use or which duality you consider first—you'll get to the core issue eventually.

Fundamentally, polarity management helps us understand that some challenges are not problems to be solved but rather tensions or paradoxes to be managed. There wasn't anything Dean could do about his father-in-law's perception of him, but he could manage interactions in a new way, set healthy boundaries, and protect his internal state from the external aggression.

The concept of polarity management applies to personal challenges as much as it does to companies, governments, institutions, and systems. For example, the polarity of "stability" and "change" is one that many organizations struggle with. Stability is important for creating a sense of continuity and consistency, but change is necessary for growth and innovation. If an organization becomes too focused on stability and resists change, it may become stagnant and fail to evolve with changing market conditions. If it becomes too focused on change and ignores the need for stability, the company may become chaotic and lose sight of its core values and mission.

Leadership is as complex as the humans in charge of it, yet we often think of leadership in binary terms. We're either great or terrible leaders, worthy or worthless, smart or stupid. There is little room for gray areas and emotional range. Of course, we sometimes experience extreme highs and lows, but most often our experience is made up of everything in between.

The Ward Model illustrates how to use self-compassion to balance and integrate opposing values, embrace ambiguity and complexity, and recognize that there are no easy answers or one-size-fits-all solutions. We learn to lose the either/or approach in favor of a both/and mindset.

FORGET "EITHER/OR"–THE WARD MODEL OFFERS A "BOTH/AND" APPROACH

It's not as complicated as it sounds. Think of breathing as a duality of inhaling and exhaling. The two actions are opposites, but you would never make the case that one is more important than the other. To survive we need to both inhale oxygen and exhale carbon dioxide. You will rarely be fully self-compassionate or fully self-abandoning, so the Ward Model encompasses the "both/and" approach at its very core. It's a model for self-compassionate leadership, teaching that it is precisely our moments of self-abandonment that give us the opportunity to change and practice self-compassion.

Polarity management doesn't mean deciding on inhaling versus exhaling. It's understanding that you need both, that they're equally valuable, and that there is a price to pay if you overindex on one or the other. The delicate balance of taking in oxygen and expelling carbon dioxide is impacted by underbreathing or holding your breath as much as it is by overbreathing or hyperventilating. Fatigue, dizziness, and inadequate blood flow to the brain are just some of the negative effects of not managing the tension between these two contrasting but equally important poles.

We're always somewhere on the spectrum, sliding up or down on the scale, skewing this way or that. At any given point, we're occupying the space of both/and, not either/or. Rather than exclusively looking backward or forward, we are moving along that timeline day to day, sometimes minute to minute. As humans, we never have a fully internal or external experience or make decisions based only on our leeward safety needs or on our most courageous windward adventures. It's always a mix of both, although we often find ourselves gravitating more in one direction than in another.

At any moment in time, you can pause and ask yourself where you stand on each of the three dualities. Are you favoring one extreme over the other? Have you skewed to one side for a while? Is it time for a course correction? Being in balance at the center of it all is purely aspirational. As flawed humans, we'll never get there. Instead, we must recognize this constant recalibration as a dynamic, flexible, ever-changing process. It's this experience of being slightly off-kilter that offers rich data for us to mine. When you notice that you're out of balance, you have an opportunity to ask yourself why.

Why do you feel stuck in the past? What are the stories keeping you from making a change for the future? Is your excessive need for financial security based on your spectacular business failure a decade ago? Are you seeking your boss's validation and accolades even if you're not quite sure whether you respect his opinion and his values don't align with yours?

EXERCISE » The Ward Model Quiz

Please rate each of the following statements on a scale of 1 to 6, where 1 is "strongly disagree" and 6 is "strongly agree."

Backward Dimension

1. I often find myself reflecting on past experiences to inform my present decisions.
2. My background and upbringing significantly shape my worldview.
3. I see value in connecting with others over shared experiences from the past.
4. I struggle with letting go of old coping mechanisms.
5. I find strength and identity in the experiences I've lived through.

Forward Dimension

1. I have a clear vision of where I want to be in the next five years.
2. The aspirations and goals of others inspire me.
3. I am driven by a purpose bigger than myself.
4. I often find myself feeling unfulfilled, thinking "I'm not there yet."

5. My personal definition of success often aligns with societal expectations.

Inward Dimension

1. I regularly take time for introspection and understand my emotions.

2. I am aware of situations or triggers that make me react impulsively.

3. I approach my feelings with curiosity rather than judgment.

4. It's easy for me to identify and express my emotions to others.

5. I often link my emotions to unmet or met personal needs.

Outward Dimension

1. I am acutely aware of how my behavior impacts those around me.

2. My actions usually align with my internal beliefs and values.

3. I ensure my words reflect my intent and am conscious of their impact on others.

4. I make it a point to be present, both mentally and emotionally, during interactions.

5. It's important for me to act in a way that offers compassion to others.

Leeward Dimension

1. I recognize when I need to step back and take care of my well-being.

2. Setting personal boundaries comes naturally to me.

3. I often find comfort in familiar habits and routines, even if they aren't always beneficial.

4. Being in nature or savoring self-care practices rejuvenates me.

5. I am comfortable taking a break in between meetings to get outside for fresh air.

Windward Dimension

1. I value experiences that challenge me and push me out of my comfort zone.

2. I am willing to take risks to achieve my goals, even if there's a chance of failure.

3. I practice self-forgiveness, especially after difficult experiences.

4. Asking for help or seeking guidance in unknown territories is important to me.

5. I often ask myself, "What if I did X, even if it scares me?"

To interpret the results, total your score for each dimension. Higher scores indicate a stronger alignment with that particular dimension. Ideally, you would find a balance between each duality (for example, backward/forward) to navigate life's polarities with self-compassion.

As you review your results, be curious rather than judgmental. There is no right or wrong test result. Your score is simply an indication of how you're balancing the dualities. As you read further, remember the directions of the Ward Model you skew toward. If you veer inward, explore what practices of outward self-compassion are available to you. If you tilt backward, get curious about how looking forward could help you develop greater self-compassion, and so on. The following chapter will dive deeper into particular practices for each pole of the Ward Model dualities.

SCALING UP THE WARD MODEL

On a foundational level, each individual must first apply the Ward Model to themselves. Leaders need to live up to their titles and model applying these concepts to everyday practice. Self-compassion allows us to accept and embrace the complexity of being human instead of attempting to fit ourselves into old binary leadership models. This means fostering an environment of open communication and collaboration, where people feel comfortable exploring different perspectives and experimenting with new approaches. By embracing the fact that as individuals we're always managing our position among the six poles or directions and within the three dualities, we can create organizations that are more resilient, adaptive, and successful in the long run.

The book *Compassionate Accountability* by my colleague Nate Regier describes how leaders often struggle to find the balance between being kind and holding people accountable.[24] Within the Ward Model, this struggle may show up as skewing too heavily windward or leeward when it comes to managing teams. These values aren't mutually exclusive but rather an example of a duality to be managed. Unrealistic standards and extreme workloads can create a harmful workplace that pushes good people away or burns them out. Being overly nice can lead to poor performance and delays. Compassionate accountability is all about forming strong relationships while also achieving your goals.

The Ward Model can scale self-compassionate leadership from individuals to teams and entire organizations. Imagine for a moment your next team huddle or project meeting in which team members share where they'd plot themselves within the Ward Model at the moment and related to the task or project at hand. Knowing where everyone on the team is positioned within the Ward Model will allow you to work together to find ways to balance and shift tasks and team members on an ongoing basis. Keep in mind that this framework is not static, like so many personality or work-style assessments, but flexible and fluid depending on the day and situational context. Whenever you plot where you or a team member are within the Ward Model, it's merely a snapshot or a starting place, never a fixed diagnosis or declaration.

Say you have an eight-person team in charge of your newest product launch. Based on individual assessments of the eight members at your last project meeting, you can see that six currently overfocus on forward versus backward, potentially prone to pushing out a minimum viable product (MVP) that's not ready to delight customers. You could provide coaching to this team to encourage deeper learning from past launches to ensure that previous experiences have been mined for data and processed to avoid future pitfalls.

Zooming out even more, you'd be able to see how teams or divisions might interact on this product launch based on where they collectively fall within the Ward Model. You might be able to find clues as to why certain teams don't work well together—for example, they may skew in opposite directions on multiple dualities. This analysis could help identify and prevent potential conflicts between departments and offer opportunities for recalibration to foster better collaboration.

All of a sudden, it might make more sense that your R&D department seems to be feuding with your marketing department. The first may include many team members who are focused inward right now because they're coming up with breakthrough ideas and need to stay in touch with their creativity, problem-solving skills, and technical knowledge. They might be so internally focused they appear siloed or shut off from other departments. This may be highly frustrating to the marketing department, which needs to communicate the benefits and advantages of your MVP to potential and existing customers in layman's terms and without a dictionary for technical jargon. They are outwardly focused on brand promotion, exposure, and tracking how customers are responding to your offerings. Helping both departments understand their differences could open up communication lines and encourage better collaboration during the launch.

Finally, on a company level, you can get an idea of big-picture themes and direction, cross-checking whether they align with your overall mission or the high-level goals you're striving to accomplish. Before a big launch or acquisition, you can take a temperature check of the company to anticipate challenges as well as double down on strengths, while guiding divisions, teams, and individuals toward rebalancing dualities if needed.

I recently worked with a client whose company was getting acquired. During such an uncertain time, everyone in the company is likely to respond differently, and their actions may show how they'd plot themselves on the leeward versus windward scale. Some individuals, teams, or entire departments may skew heavily leeward, resisting the change, worried about losing their jobs, or ignoring what's happening altogether. Knowing this, you can brainstorm as a company about how you might reorient windward by inspiring excitement and optimism about potential growth, new challenges, and opportunities.

The Ward Model itself embodies self-compassion and is a tool not for judging individuals, teams, divisions, or companies but for inspiring a deeper level of self-reflection. It offers an opportunity to discover what's contributing to wherever we're currently plotted within the model without declaring a rigid and permanent assessment, like so many other personality or work-style frameworks. From there, we can deploy self-compassion at every level of the organization to validate experiences while encouraging recalibration toward balance, if what is needed is a more well-rounded approach, team, or department. In some instances, you may deliberately choose to forgo balance in service of a big project or push that requires you to skew heavier windward, outward, and forward than leeward, inward, and backward.

There is no wrong or right answer, only an agile model that waxes and wanes just like you and your company, shows you where you are right now, and signals which direction you need to go to reach your goal. This self-compassionate leadership approach is built into the Ward Model itself, honoring the humanity and constantly evolving nature of everyone contributing to the ever-changing mosaic of your company or cause.

In essence, the Ward Model highlights the inherent tensions that come with balancing between our competing needs and wants. We become aware by mindfully looking inward to understand the quality of our being, so we can align our outward expression. We accept our common humanity by looking backward to reflect on our experiences, so we can move forward with vision. We navigate our windward rock-bottom moments with self-kindness, so we can balance our safety needs with accountability to act courageously and dream big.

The Ward Model offers a flexible framework for being fully human while striving for excellence as a leader. In the next three chapters, we'll delve deeper into each of the three dualities that teach us awareness, acceptance, and accountability to become truly self-compassionate leaders.

4 » AWARENESS

Balancing Being and Doing

> If you are distressed by anything external, the pain
> is not due to the thing itself, but to your estimate
> of it; and this you have the power to revoke at any
> moment.
>
> MARCUS AURELIUS, Roman emperor
> and stoic philosopher

I lay sprawled out on my living room floor in the middle of the day, crying uncontrollably, tears sliding down the sides of my face and onto the carpet. The shortness of breath, tension in my chest, and tightness in my stomach felt like a heart attack. The overwhelming anxiety constricted my throat and choked my sobs. Although I felt the floor beneath me, I felt as though I was untethered from reality. The floor was not a foundation but an edge I could slide off of any second, falling from the face of the Earth.

It was spring 2020, the start of the pandemic, and I was terrified. Although I had struggled with depression and anxiety throughout my life, this feeling of uncontrolled panic was new, and I'd never experienced such a severe breakdown. The depth of my sadness scared me. Suicidal thoughts and profound hopelessness made me feel lost, alone, and out of control. The months leading up to this moment were fraught with uncertainty for people all around the world as we began navigating lockdowns, remote schooling, and working from home. My role running the global leadership development team for Slalom was beginning to unravel. I was excellent at being an individual contributor (IC) and thrived as a facilitator and coach. Unfortunately, as the 360 assessment had pointed out, I was not a great manager. I gave up the responsibility of managing people to build a new coaching and high-performance team methodology for the organization. I felt surrounded by misinformation, misdirection, and manipulation. I didn't know which way was up and what parts of the chaos were my responsibility. I wanted to help and fix—but also control and direct—the situation to make everything okay again. The more I tried, however, the worse the problems became.

Fortunately, my wife, Brie, was by my side for support. As I lay there on my living room floor, shrouded in shame and tears, Brie shared with me a passage from Glennon Doyle's memoir *Untamed*, hoping the words would soothe and ground me: "Since I got sober, I have never been fine again, not for a single moment. I have been exhausted and terrified and angry. I have been overwhelmed and underwhelmed and debilitatingly depressed and anxious. I have been amazed and awed and delighted and overjoyed to bursting. I have been reminded, constantly, by the Ache: This will pass; stay close. I have been alive."[25]

While my struggle was not with sobriety, Glennon's words in that moment were a reminder that I was not alone. I knew I was loved and would get through this painful experience. I was reminded of the power of self-compassion. I share the experience of suffering with all of humanity. These difficult feelings are a part of life, and I have the power to be kind to myself. Revisiting this mantra of self-compassion gave me clarity in the fog of emotional overload. I called my therapist, whom I'd seen on and off for nearly twenty years. I'm forever grateful that, during this proverbial dark night of my soul, this man who'd walked with me for two decades continued to be a guiding light.

After several therapy sessions it became obvious that I needed to take a leave of absence to focus on my mental health. I felt guilty and weak for needing this time off, thinking of all the people I knew who had been through worse during the pandemic. I fully understood that it was a privilege to take this time off work, and yet it was essential. Otherwise, I was genuinely scared of causing physical harm to myself.

My employer graciously allowed me six weeks. I was hopeful this time would allow me to regain my footing and get back on solid ground. Had I known what awaited me upon my return to work, I might have decided to repress my needs instead.

REPRESSING YOUR NEEDS IS NOT GOOD LEADERSHIP—IT'S RECKLESS

Many executives I've worked with fear losing their competitive edge when starting a self-compassion practice. They're used to ignoring or repressing their physical sensations, emotions, and thoughts, thinking it makes them faster, better, and stronger, when the opposite is often true. We frequently forget the real consequences of this type of "leadership" approach.

The high-stakes, high-pressure executive office isn't just a place of power but, as research suggests, a potential hotbed of health issues. It's like sitting at the helm of a ship during a storm. The view is unmatched, but so is the stress. A study published in the *Journal of Applied Psychology* reveals that organizational leaders, despite their seemingly extensive resources, are more prone to anxiety and depression than other people.[26] The stress of making crucial decisions, dealing with organizational politics, and managing interpersonal conflicts can take a toll.

The *Harvard Business Review* reported that nearly 50 percent of leaders experience burnout.[27] The demands of leadership can also translate into tangible physical health risks, like heart attacks. A study published in the *Scandinavian Journal of Work, Environment and Health* finds that high job demands increase the risk of heart attack by almost 50 percent[28]—a staggering number. The American Heart Association has also identified a clear correlation between work-related stress and the risk of stroke.[29] The higher the demands and the lower a person's level of control (a common paradox in leadership), the higher the risk.

We're expected to stay stoic in the face of challenges, act even-keeled in chaos, and show no weakness. What we miss is a treasure trove of data points, flashing red arrows, and signposts that could help us understand ourselves better and

FIGURE 4. The Inward/Outward Duality. How do we leverage
mindful awareness so we can look inward to improve our
quality of being, which will reflect in our outward expression of
leadership?

prevent serious physical and mental health problems, if only
we paid attention with curiosity rather than judgment.

When it comes to gaining awareness by looking inward,
consider three main dimensions:

» Gut: your physical quality of being

» Heart: your emotional quality of being

» Mind: your mental quality of being

All three form the basis of mindful awareness of your internal state, which impacts how you interact and engage with
the outside world, as a human and as a leader (figures 4 and 5).

GUT: YOUR PHYSICAL QUALITY OF BEING

In a culture where we're taught to live as "heads-on-sticks" instead of fully embodied humans, it makes sense that we often
pay no attention to our bodily sensations during work. We
can power through a twelve-hour day without eating lunch,
no problem. We don't even have time to use the restroom because we've scheduled back-to-back meetings for hours on
end.

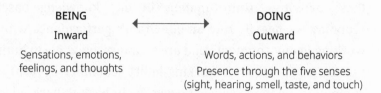

BEING	DOING
Inward	Outward
Sensations, emotions, feelings, and thoughts	Words, actions, and behaviors Presence through the five senses (sight, hearing, smell, taste, and touch)

FIGURE 5. Gaining Balance between Being and Doing. The duality of being/doing corresponds to the inward/outward on-ramps for the Ward Model and represents awareness.

Embodiment is becoming aware of your inward experience by connecting to your body's sensations, such as increasing heart rate, accelerated breathing, or sweaty palms, which then inform your outward interactions. Maybe embodiment and taking care of your physical needs sounds a bit woo-woo. But is it really dumber than relying on Adderall or legal stimulants to get your work done, taking the edge off by getting buzzed every night, or having a stress-induced heart attack in your fifties?

Athletes take care of their bodies because they know it's the foundation for peak performance. And while most business leaders aren't professional athletes, the way we take care of our physical needs affects our emotions, moods, and cognitive performance.

Your Brain Needs Oxygen and Movement

Your brain makes up one-fifteenth of your body weight but uses nearly one-fifth of total available oxygen.[30] Oxygen is essential for learning and processing, so moving oxygen to your brain consistently is one of the primary ways to maximize those activities. Unfortunately, in our knowledge-based economy we heavily rely on our brain's performance while working in environments that are counterproductive to brain health. We spend most working hours sedentary in front of computers, on video calls, at desks, or in back-to-back meetings. After just twenty to thirty minutes of sitting, about 80 percent of blood pools in our hips.[31] Having only 20 percent of blood left to carry oxygen to your brain negatively impacts your cognition and executive functioning.

The antidote to that brain slump is movement. Eric Jensen and Liesl McConchie's book *Brain-Based Learning: The New Paradigm of Teaching* states that movement facilitates learning by creating a greater number of synapses, or neural connections, in the brain.[32] Getting up every half hour to get some water, use the restroom, or stretch for a few minutes can help, but the study clearly shows that longer, more consistent movement is key. This may explain why you prefer working out a problem with a colleague while standing at a whiteboard, find walking meetings to be more productive than sitting across a conference table, and don't experience as much brain fatigue since getting your treadmill desk.

Your Brain and Your Gut: Best Friends Forever

You may have heard your gut referred to as your second brain, but why? Gastroenterologist and *New York Times* best-selling author of the book *Fiber Fueled*, Will Bulsiewicz, explains that while our brain has approximately 100 billion neurons, the organ with the second-highest concentration of neurons, with approximately 500 million of them, is the gut.[33]

Your nervous system connects your gut and brain via the vagus nerve, which sends and receives signals both ways. An animal study included in *Fiber Fueled* showed that stress in-hibits signals sent through the vagus nerve, causing gastroin-testinal problems. For example, if people are scared to death and lose control of their bowel or bladder, it's because of the break in neural connection between the brain, the intestines, and the gut. You can probably think of plenty of examples yourself. Maybe you routinely get stomach cramps or heart-burn before an important presentation, product launch, or performance review.

Your gut health can also impact your mood and sleep pat-terns because many neurotransmitters, such as serotonin (one of the "happy" hormones), are produced in the gut. The production of serotonin depends on the number and types of microbes that live in your gut, which are dependent on a host of factors, including the foods you eat and medications you take.

Mood swings, lack of sleep, and stress-induced physical symptoms can all keep you from being the high-performing leader you want to be. Ignoring these physical symptoms works temporarily, but sooner or later you'll have to deal with the fallout. If you can't regulate your mood and blow up at your team, you'll end up in the HR office. If you constantly operate on a lack of sleep, you'll eventually make a big mis-take that will cost your company money.

All these physical systems have an impact on our emotional and mental states, our feelings and ideas, and our cognitive performance.

Sleep: Your Most Underrated Superpower

You can survive for several weeks without food and up to a week without water, but you can only go without sleep for a few days. The American National Sleep Foundation recommends that everyone between the ages of sixteen and sixty-four get seven to nine hours of sleep every night. Even light sleep deprivation can impair logical reasoning, executive functioning, and attention. More severe sleep deprivation can lead to anxiety, depression, and even paranoia in extreme cases.[34]

I won't give you a list of dos and don'ts, especially because I'm struggling with implementing a healthy sleep routine too. However, there is great advice out there to experiment with, such as cutting alcohol and coffee, quitting eating two hours before bed to reduce sugar spikes and blood flow activation, and limiting screen time to keep the blue light from suppressing the pineal gland that produces melatonin (which makes us drowsy). In addition to these practical ideas, we must also address our culture's obsession with grinding and hustling at the expense of sleep and rest.

HEART: YOUR EMOTIONAL QUALITY OF BEING

Think of emotions as primary, basic human expressions based on physical processes, such as hormones and neurological activities. Our bodies react through pupil dilation, sweating, or an elevated heart rate. Feelings are the secondary expressions of those emotions and are defined by the meaning we make and the stories we tell ourselves about experiencing that primary emotion.

Emotions and feelings are tightly connected, of course, but it's helpful to remember that our emotions are based on physical processes and our feelings are triggered by our mental framing of a situation and experience of the emotion in context. A 2015 study by Debra Trampe and two coauthors observed emotions in everyday life by prompting study participants to report on their emotional state at random times. The researchers found that participants experienced at least one emotion 90 percent of the time.[35] The top three reported emotions were joy, love, and anxiety, and people described feeling positive emotions 2.5 times more frequently than negative ones. Participants commonly experienced both positive and negative emotions simultaneously—the paradox of bittersweetness. This study shows that at any given point in time you're likely to feel an emotion, and often a mix of contradicting emotions.

What we do with these complex emotions throughout our day is incredibly important. In Susan David's foundational book *Emotional Agility*, she explains that acknowledging and accepting our feelings as they are and without judgment causes them to dissipate rather than becoming an endless loop of feelings about our emotions.[36] I personally use a slightly different term, "emotional fluency," because it reminds me of learning to speak a new language by identifying, experiencing, and expressing emotions with curiosity and compassion.

While it's common to disregard our emotions and instead pretend we can just get over them, we really don't. Emotions that aren't acknowledged or accepted take on a life of their own. They shift your focus away from the conversation, meeting, or project you're now half-assing as you spend most of your energy ruminating about that frustrating argument with your coworker last week.

Feelings about Our Feelings

Emotions are rarely what keep us from moving on with our day. Having feelings about those original emotions without processing them is where the trouble starts.

Susan David's approach is to deal with the primary emotions, identifying and naming them to give ourselves time to process them. Of course, this is more difficult when we lack emotional fluency. In a study with 7,000 participants conducted over five years, Brené Brown and her team discovered that, on average, individuals could only recognize three emotions while experiencing them: happiness, sadness, and anger.[37] Only being able to identify "glad, sad, mad" is woefully insufficient. Imagine trying to navigate the world with a vocabulary of three words—it would be near impossible to find your way around, build relationships, or access food and shelter. And yet many of us accept that we're the equivalent of a crying baby or a toddler in a tantrum when it comes to communicating our feelings. Most of us have never been taught the language of emotions, so we're not proficient in understanding and speaking it. This is why developing emotional fluency is so important. The language of our emotions connects us to our humanity, our needs, our purpose, and one another.

When learning the language of emotions and working on our fluency, it's helpful to have a dictionary of commonly used phrases or, in this case, commonly felt emotions. Take a look at the list of the seven most common emotions and their closely associated, but much more specific, feelings (figure 6). Working with this list can help us build emotional fluency by identifying and understanding our emotional landscapes in more depth.

Happy

Aroused	Hopeful	Optimistic	Proud
Confident	Interested	Peaceful	Thankful
Content	Joyful	Playful	

Sad

Abandoned	Disappointed	Hurt	Powerless
Ashamed	Grief-stricken	Inferior	Vulnerable
Depressed	Guilty	Lonely	

Bad

Apathetic	Indifferent	Skeptical	Unfocused
Bored	Overwhelmed	Stressed	Worthless
Busy	Pressured	Tired	

Mad

Aggressive	Bitter	Frustrated	Provoked
Angry	Critical	Hostile	Ridiculed
Betrayed	Disrespected	Jealous	

Fearful

Alarmed	Frightened	Nervous	Scared
Anxious	Helpless	Panicky	Threatened
Exposed	Insecure	Rejected	

Surprised

Amazed	Confused	Excited	Startled
Astonished	Dumbfounded	Perplexed	Stunned
Bewildered	Energetic	Shocked	

Disgusted

Appalled	Hesitant	Offended	Repulsed
Disapproving	Judgmental	Outraged	Sickened
Embarrassed	Nauseated	Repelled	

FIGURE 6. Seven Most Common Emotions and Their Related Feelings. Practice emotional fluency by identifying and understanding your specific feelings in more depth.

In an ideal situation, when we process emotions as they arise, we can move through them quickly instead of creating more and more ripples in the form of secondary feelings that keep us awake at night and stewing for weeks. Psychologist Daniel Goleman coined the "six-second rule," referring to the idea that it takes about six seconds to regain emotional regulation after being triggered by a stressful or emotional event.[38] If we don't use mindful self-awareness to interrupt the automatic physiological response to stress, we experience what is often called amygdala hijacking, when our brain's survival instinct plunges us into a fight, flight, freeze, or fawn response. Whether you take a deep breath, count to ten, do a grounding exercise, or reframe extreme thoughts, creating that small buffer between stimulus and response actively calms your nervous system.

Susan David explains that we speak about 16,000 words a day.[39] Imagine how many unspoken words race through our minds on any given day. Most of them are not fact-based but rather judgments and evaluations attached to an emotion. The unspoken words, or internal monologues, are where we make up the stories and judgments about our emotions, relationships, and situations. These constant judgments frequently result in so many layers of feelings that we no longer know why we feel a certain way and what sparked the original feeling. Although we commonly use our internal monologue to quash uncomfortable or negative emotions, several studies have shown that suppression only amplifies those emotions.

Harvard professor Daniel Wegner asked participants in a study to avoid thinking about white bears.[40] Of course, they couldn't stop thinking about white bears. Even after the prohibition was lifted, participants continued to think about white bears much more than the control group. The same happens when we try to suppress our emotions. Denying, minimizing, or repressing them will only make them more intense and long-lasting. The key is to neither suppress them nor buy into them as if they were facts. Self-compassion can help us identify and acknowledge these emotions without judgment, so that we can process them quickly and move on—which brings us back to the practice of emotional fluency.

Reddit founder Alexis Ohanian shared his own practice on the *Imposters* podcast after working with an executive coach.[41] Ohanian learned the power of pausing between stimulus and response so he could acknowledge and name his emotion instead of repressing it. Especially with highly-charged emotions, such as anger, this process allowed him to defang the emotion and hone the ability to ask: Hey anger, I see you—what are you trying to tell me?

Emotions Are Signposts to Guide Us

I agree with Susan David that we are not our emotions, but identifying, labeling, and processing them does help us understand who we are and what's going on in our lives. Emotions often signal that something important is at stake or that one of our core values isn't being honored. If you feel lonely at work, you may be tempted to suppress that feeling. If, however, you allow yourself to experience the loneliness, chances are you'll realize that feeling lonely can be an important indicator of issues you need to resolve because one of your values is connection and belonging.

Only once you allow yourself to accept and feel the loneliness can you start figuring out your next step. Maybe you need to get more involved at your place of work. Or maybe it's not the right workplace for you because the organization doesn't value connection among its staff. Maybe you need to invest more in your relationships outside of work so that your expectations of work relationships are more reasonable. Maybe you need a combination of these steps, or something entirely different. Regardless of what you need to do next, you will not find out unless you fully allow yourself to feel the feeling first. The important thing is to slow yourself down enough to examine the reality of the situation with compassion. What is going on for you, both internally and externally, that needs to be addressed?

Because we're so focused on either repressing uncomfortable feelings or fixing them, it's tempting to jump to a conclusion. What do I do? What are the three easy steps to fix this problem? But the steps to fixing whatever issue your emotion is surfacing are highly specific to you and your situation. The work of leveraging self-compassion to accept your emotions rather than attempt to control them is not a quick fix. It takes time, effort, and curiosity to navigate through each individual situation rather than slapping a one-size-fits-all process on each challenge. In my experience, this customized approach is well worth the effort, because it helps us pinpoint which situations, relationships, and actions are not aligned with our values and purpose and why.

You may sometimes feel lost in your emotions or overwhelmed by the prospect of having to find your way through the chaos inside. It can feel like trying to safely steer a ship through a terrifying storm. Think of your destination as your overarching life goals, and the horizon and celestial bodies as your core values and purpose. You must bring your ship (yourself) in alignment with your values and purpose to reach your destination (goal). When you're lost in a storm or trying to find your way in the darkness (difficult and complex emotions), you'll hone your strength, resilience, and capabilities steering your ship, while the horizon and north star (your values and purpose) orient you and help you safely navigate through the storm.

Emotions change like the weather, but values provide you with a steadfast guide.

EXERCISE » Notice, Name, Need, Next Step—How to Navigate Chaotic Emotional States

The reasons we default to repressing or minimizing emotions are varied. Sometimes we've been conditioned to do so; sometimes we've had a bad experience expressing vulnerability or don't believe we are capable of facing certain emotions or dealing with them in a productive way. Self-compassion can help us navigate these choppy waters. Using a fictional case study, let's practice processing an emotion with the 4Ns:

1. **Notice:** Practice mindful awareness to recognize emotions as they arise.

2. **Name:** Identify your specific emotion (use the emotion/feelings list in figure 6 if it's helpful).

3. **Need:** Determine how the emotion connects to your values and illustrates what you need in the moment.

4. **Next step:** Identify what action you can take to meet
   your need.

Notice: Practice mindful awareness to recognize emotions
as they arise.

Without your consent or knowledge, your teammate completed a shared project, disregarding your input or contribution, and you were blindsided in a meeting. Notice the basic,
primary emotion you're experiencing and the physical sensations, such as sweating, increased heart rate, tears, or muscle tension, that accompany it. While you're sitting through
the presentation, you try to keep it together as you feel your
cheeks flush, your throat constrict, and your eyes well up.

Name: Identify your specific emotion.

You identify your primary emotions as surprise (you were
blindsided) and anger (your contribution was ignored). As
you dig a little deeper, you discover feelings of confusion and
betrayal (related to the primary emotion of surprise). You also
recognize that you feel insulted and provoked (related to the
primary emotion of anger).

Need: Determine how the emotion connects to your values
and illustrates what you need in the moment.

Two of your central values are inclusion and respect. You understand that this situation violates both values because your
colleague did not consider your input into the project, went
behind your back instead of confronting you directly, and
made you look uninformed and out of the loop in the meeting.
You need to feel like a valued member of the team.

Next step: Identify what action you can take to meet your need.

You excuse yourself and duck into the restroom right as your tears spill out (or as you're swallowing hard to force them back down). This is the point where you might start telling yourself to suck it up and either repress your emotions or get revenge. Instead, you breathe, compose yourself, and consider your options for next steps. Instead of aggressively confronting your teammate in the meeting, you decide to go back, listen and take notes, and then ask for a one-on-one conversation with your teammate afterward. Of course, the conversation itself will give you more data on steps to take in the future. Maybe it was all a misunderstanding. Maybe your teammate purposely excluded you but will take responsibility for their actions so you can salvage your working relationship. Maybe you'll realize this team isn't a good fit for you.

The more you practice this exercise, the more comfortable you will become in feeling your feelings, using them as data points to recognize unmet needs, and aligning your response with your core values.

All Feelings Are for Feeling

Once you start observing your feelings, you may find that you're quite comfortable having and identifying certain feelings but not others. Although we often talk about "positive" or "negative" emotions, when it comes to understanding our feelings, they're all neutral. All feelings are for feeling, and you don't need to judge yourself for having certain emotions and feelings instead of others. Whether you repress joy or pain, the repression will cause damage, just in different ways. Whether you prefer anger over sadness or the other way around, you won't be able to experience your full humanity if you restrict your range of feelings. Emotional agility, as explained by Susan David, means not only allowing feelings but also allowing *all* feelings without judgment. Similarly, my concept of emotional fluency focuses on being curious about our emotions so we can be well versed in all of them instead of trying to find our way through life with only a few vocabulary words.

Some emotions will be more difficult to allow than others. That's normal. Often we're culturally conditioned to find certain emotions more acceptable for men (anger) or women (sadness) or have been taught by our families that some feelings are childish (wonder) or weak (desperation). Emotions are not assigned by gender, cultural or familial background, race, ethnicity, religion, or anything else. All emotions are part of the human experience, and we're all human. When feelings arise that you have been taught to repress, be extra gentle with yourself. Some feelings will bring up more shame and denial than others if we believe we're not meeting someone else's standard, fulfilling our roles, or embarrassing our family, community, or country.

There is no easy way out of this conditioning, other than becoming aware that the emotions that trigger an intense internal response of their own will require an extra dose of self-compassion while you process them. Doing this hard work is worth it. Getting more comfortable with our emotional states is invaluable in learning how they impact our mental states and patterns of thought.

MIND: YOUR MENTAL QUALITY OF BEING

Imagine you're sitting in a room without your phone. There's no TV either, no magazines or books, no pictures on the wall, no windows, no other people. Just you on that chair for fifteen minutes. In the corner is a device that will deliver an electric shock if you push a button. What will you do? Keep yourself company in your own head or distract yourself with painful electric shocks?

An experiment just like this was designed by Timothy Wilson and his colleagues to find out what participants do when left alone without distractions for periods of six to fifteen minutes. Astonishingly, the experiment published in *Science* reported that 67 percent of men and 25 percent of women found being alone with themselves so unpleasant that they ended up self-inducing electric shocks. One man even shocked himself 190 times.[42] It's surprising how many of us would rather experience pain than be left alone with our thoughts. What's going on in our minds that makes it so unbearable for us to hang out there?

In recovery circles, people are often reminded not to believe everything they think. As a society, we've established a hierarchy of sorts that posits we should value and believe our thoughts over our emotions. Especially in high-performance leadership circles, we pride ourselves on being rational, logical, and analytical. Often, though, our thoughts are as confusing, misleading, or unhelpful as our emotions can be in identifying the facts of a situation or making a decision.

Self-compassion helps us observe both with curiosity and distance. Our thoughts and emotions influence each other, and probing one will likely bring up the other.

Storytime in Your Brain

In a conversation, author Adam Grant presented Nobel Prize–winning psychologist Daniel Kahneman with new information that contradicted one of Kahneman's long-held beliefs. The conversation was included in Adam Grant's book *Think Again*, where Grant explains how to navigate two common biases—confirmation bias and desirability bias.[43] We encounter confirmation bias when we see what we expect to see and desirability bias when we see what we want to see. Both can trip us up, trapping us in stories rather than helping us deal with reality as it is.

The point here is not the specific new information conveyed during the conversation, but rather Kahneman's reaction to it: he was elated to be wrong. He was delighted to find an opportunity to learn something new. Kahneman is undoubtedly brilliant, but it appears that his life and career also owe much to his curiosity and deep love of learning. He is clearly thrilled to question his beliefs and test his assumptions because he knows he ultimately benefits by gaining more knowledge. If you can prioritize learning over being right, you will have a much easier time challenging your own biases as they arise and thereby achieving continued evolution and growth, both personally and professionally. Absorbing and adapting to new information is one of the hallmarks of great leaders because it keeps them agile rather than stuck in their old ways.

EXERCISE » **Red-Flag Thoughts**

There are many models and frameworks explaining how to spot faulty thinking patterns, and you could spend months reading all the books on this topic. Some of them are so detailed that they can be more confusing than clarifying. I've found it helpful to focus on two faulty patterns that have been major red flags in my own thinking: rigid black-and-white thinking that turns into limiting labels and repetitive stories.

Limiting Labels

Black-and-white thinking leaves no room for gray areas and nuance; thoughts are extreme and inflexible. Watch out for always/never thoughts: *I always screw up. I'm never going to get that job. I always say something stupid in meetings. I never speak up for my team.*

» Write down five always/never statements about yourself as they come to mind. Are they factually true? Did they originate with you? In other words, can you pinpoint a situation that made you believe this thought for the first time? Did they originate with someone else? Where did you hear them first (your teacher, your parent, your spouse)?

» How can you reframe these statements with more self-compassion and nuance? Your well-intentioned, misinformed protector (WIMP) might think: *I always screw up.* A compassionate reframe would be: *I struggled on this project, because I'm still learning the skills required*

for this position. Learning from these errors will prepare
me for the next project.

Repetitive Stories

Say your parents used to joke about how clumsy you were as
a kid. Now, as an adult, when you knock over a glass or trip
on the carpet, you immediately call up the familiar stories of
being a klutz regardless of whether you're actually clumsier
than anyone else. These thoughts that turned into stories
and then family lore can make us believe this is who we are,
whether it's the klutz or the clown, the screw-up or the golden
child, the bossy bitch or the doormat, the mama's boy or the
daddy's girl.

» Write down the first three stories about you that come to
  mind (either stories you tell about yourself or the kind
  you suffer through at every family holiday). Are they true?
  How have they affected what you think about yourself,
  who you believe you are at your core, or what you can
  accomplish? Is there a specific origin to each story you can
  remember?

» Can you reframe the story or separate those thoughts/
  behaviors from your identity now? Your WIMP might
  think: *I'm a klutz.* A compassionate reframe would be:
  Whether or not I was clumsy as a child doesn't mean I am
  now as an adult. Even if I was more prone to accidents, that
  doesn't diminish my value or worth.

Never Leave Your Thoughts Unattended

Researchers have found that our thoughts wander nearly half of our waking hours.[44] What would happen if we were able to be more present with our thoughts instead of allowing our minds to meander aimlessly? How would that presence affect our well-being, effectiveness, and work performance? How many times have you walked out of a meeting thinking everyone was on the same page, only to realize later that somehow every attendee made up a different story in their head or didn't remember what was said in the same way?

Knowing that all our minds get sidetracked half the time (and not all at the same time) makes it obvious why people can come out of meetings or conversations with completely different ideas about what happened. When we consider that our thoughts become words, then actions, habits, character, and finally our reality, it's even more crucial to understand that half of the time we give up ownership of that first domino, our thoughts.

Thoughts » Words » Actions » Habits » Character = Reality

What happens in our mind creates our reality—not because of magic, but because our thoughts constantly influence our emotions, decisions, and actions, creating a ripple effect that runs throughout our lives. As the writer Anaïs Nin said, "We don't see things as they are, we see them as we are." This process also works backward. When we question our perspective on the world, other people, or ourselves, we can backtrack to find the thoughts, ideas, and stories that are the origin of our perspectives, attitudes, and opinions.

Deploying self-compassion to withhold self-judgment creates a space where we can recognize the patterns, triggers, and stories that we consistently get stuck in or ruminate on, so we can initiate change or let go of that behavior. When we interrupt judgmental self-labeling (*I'm a failure / a fraud / bad / less than*) to humanize and treat ourselves with compassion instead (*I did the best I could / I will learn from this experience*), we can pause old behavioral patterns and make a different choice in the moment.

Once we become attuned in that way, we can begin the work of dismantling the stories that no longer serve us, the ideas not based on fact, and the thoughts that hold us back. This practice also allows us to become more flexible and thoughtful in our interactions with others and honor our differences. Knowing that we all live in unique realities based on our distinct perspectives on the facts teaches us to communicate more intentionally to close that gap as much as possible.

WOO-WOO WINS » Brian

My client Brian didn't like to take up space in meetings. He was a regional general manager for an insurance company, slated to be put in charge of the entire West Coast. The company's executive team believed in his capabilities, but Brian lacked confidence in himself, and this insecurity came out as people-pleaser and imposter WIMPs. He looked enviously at "strong leaders" who spoke up with conviction in meetings, owned the room, and acted confident and outgoing. Meanwhile, he stammered and stopped breathing whenever he was in a situation where he feared being judged. He started to question his expertise and knowledge and wondered whether he had anything to contribute because he couldn't be like those other leaders.

Brian and I discussed how bringing our full selves to our lives doesn't mean being like other people or squeezing ourselves into a mold that doesn't fit our personality and style. I reminded Brian that he had a valuable perspective and skill set and deserved a place at the table and a voice in every meeting. There was no need for him to become an outspoken leader full of bravado. Instead, he needed to work on valuing himself so he could be grounded in what he personally had to offer.

Brian started by reframing the "backward" story that he didn't belong in his position, listing his past accomplishments, strengths, and experiences that made him qualified for the role and highlighted his unique value proposition to the senior leadership team. He recognized that the story he'd been telling himself was not only wrong but also deprived the business of all he had to offer. When he realized he had a diverse skill set and valuable experience, he understood he was doing the company a disservice by staying quiet. Instead of fearing that if he spoke up, he would be seen as grandstanding, obnoxious, or attention seeking, he allowed for the possibility that his team valued his contributions.

I challenged Brian to conduct a micro-experiment where he would speak up and test his new assumption. Would he be appreciated for adding value or seen as a distraction? He set up one-on-one meetings with peers to build closer relationships and learn what their respective markets were working on. He pushed himself to speak up early in senior leadership meetings and get the discomfort out of the way, leading to more natural exchanges. Finally, at a question-and-answer session during the annual leadership meeting, he made it a point to ask the CEO a question in front of his peers from across the country. Each of the micro-experiments helped Brian change the story he'd told himself. Through multiple situations, meetings, and feedback, he learned that his questions were insightful, his ideas appreciated, and his contributions valued.

Power posing, breathwork, or reciting mantras may or may not work for you. That's not my point. Instead of selling you a fake silver bullet, I want you to be open to valuing and trusting yourself enough to experiment with what works for you and then unapologetically be yourself. And it all starts with being aware of what's happening inside your body, including taking care of your brain.

EXERCISE » One-Week Mantra Challenge for Fellow Cynics

If the words "mantra" or "affirmations" make you roll your eyes, let me challenge you to try this out for one week. I used to think it was absolutely ridiculous to put my hand on my heart and recite my custom mantras to myself in difficult moments, but it works. The ones I currently use are:

» I, Massimo, am a work in progress.

» Don't judge yourself, others, or the process.

» I am loved, loving, and lovable.

» Surrender and abundance.

Borrow one of mine or make up your own. You may find it
helpful to create a mantra for addressing a well-intentioned,
misinformed protector (WIMP) you keep running into.
Here are some examples of WIMP-centric mantras:

» **Perfectionist:** I'm good enough exactly as I am.

» **Hard-ass:** I deserve rest and relaxation.

» **Achiever:** My worth lies in who I am, not what I can do
   for others.

» **People pleaser:** It's okay to disappoint others instead of
   betraying myself.

» **Imposter:** I'm accepted, appreciated, and respected for my
   true self.

» **Contrarian:** There's nothing to prove.

Maybe it feels more important to create a mantra for an
emotion that keeps coming up that you have a hard time accepting or processing.
Here are some examples of emotion-centric mantras:

» Anger is an important activating emotion that shows me
   my boundaries.

» I deserve joy and ease.

» I can hold my grief without letting it overwhelm me.

Instructions: Repeat the mantra/s to yourself every day for a
week and see what happens. Try to be curious and let go of
expectations.

Kristin Neff, university professor and author of the foundational work *Self-Compassion* is widely credited for explaining that the first step in practicing self-compassion is allowing ourselves to feel all feelings without judgment and to become aware of our pain as it is, without attempting to repress, deny, or minimize it.[45] Neff encourages us to talk to ourselves like we would speak to a good friend we care about and love. "I'm a failure" turns into "I'm doing the best I can right now," and "I'm the only one who struggles with XYZ" becomes "Others have experienced similar feelings and challenges." Speaking to ourselves with compassion is the first step in becoming a better leader. Soon, you'll find yourself modeling self-compassion to your team with transformational results.

LEVERAGE YOUR QUALITY OF BEING AS A LEADER

Kelly broke down in tears fifteen minutes before the start of a leadership program we were co-facilitating. It wasn't the event itself that *caused* the tears; rather, it was the space we created as a team that *allowed* the tears. Before every session, we huddled together as a team, and each of us answered these three questions:

1. How do you feel?
2. What do you need?
3. What updates do you have to share?

Kelly started crying when answering the question about how she was feeling. It was an essential lesson in practicing what I preach. I could not facilitate a workshop on the importance of emotionally intelligent leadership if I couldn't support my own teammate in sharing her authentic experience.

Kelly, a passionate project manager on the team, felt anxious about the workshop and struggled with her imposter WIMP, questioning her skills and talent for the work she was there to do. When we asked her what she needed, she requested reassurance about her role on the team. Crammed tightly into a conference room at a Nashville hotel, each team member reflected on their genuine appreciation for Kelly as a person and respected colleague. Her mood shifted almost instantly, and she regained her spark, getting fired up and ready to stand in her power for the workshop that was about to start.

That's the power of leveraging your own quality of being as a leader, which allows you to be present for yourself and everyone around you. Creating a space that welcomes vulnerability and genuine engagement can transform your working relationships. It may sound like Kelly's feelings could have derailed the entire workshop, when in reality we simply required a few minutes of deep and focused attention on our own and each other's feelings. What actually could have derailed the workshop was a team member repressing their valid emotions and thus limiting their capacity to be their best and truest self.

It takes a lot of trust and courage to allow yourself to be seen like that, but it's exactly what we need as individuals, teams, and society. We need to relearn how to tap into that inner knowing and then have the guts to share it with others. Sometimes we're so focused on optimizing everything that we optimize humanity out of our interactions. Focusing on our

INWARD/BEING	OUTWARD/DOING
Who you are	What you've done
Personal growth	Accomplishments
Lead self	Lead others
Intent	Impact
Self-reflection	Action
Character	Reputation
Eulogy virtues	Résumé virtues

FIGURE 7. Inward/Being and Outward/Doing. The tension of inward/being and outward/doing can look like this in practice.

physical, emotional, and mental state of being can offer an understanding of our needs and curiosity about other people's needs that gives us the confidence to lead not with research statistics, but with humanity.

For example, I give a heads-up to all my workshop and training participants that I'm happy to hug at the end of the day when we all go our separate ways; if they're more comfortable with a handshake, they should just extend their hand instead. Obviously, personal preferences and consent are key, which is why I have the conversation at the beginning of our time together. Hugging is my preference, and I feel a good embrace can be cathartic, create a deeper connection, and reduce stress. A 2021 study by Anna L. Dueren et al. reports that hugs lasting between five and ten seconds are rated more highly than shorter hugs.[46] What does it say that we're now studying the optimal length for hugging?

This is not to say that we should or shouldn't hug or that the study findings are wrong. It is interesting, however, that we don't trust ourselves enough to tap into our gut, heart, and mind to figure out what type of connection would feel good at the moment and to communicate that to others directly and specifically. Working on becoming aware of our inward states and how they affect our outward behaviors will allow us to balance the tension between being and doing (figure 7).

When we use the Ward Model to help us figure out where we are on the duality of inward and outward, being and doing, we gain awareness, which is the essential foundation for attaining the next layer of self-compassionate leadership—acceptance.

5 » ACCEPTANCE

Understanding Context and Clarity

> Because one believes in oneself, one doesn't try to
> convince others. Because one is content with one-
> self, one doesn't need others' approval. Because one
> accepts oneself, the whole world accepts him or her.
>
> LAO TZU, Taoist philosopher

Everyone was on the edge of their seat, intently listening to
Mehrsa, one of my workshop attendees. She was a successful
corporate attorney who typically had a tough, capable demeanor with an air of detachment. But now, she was sharing
stories about growing up in an immigrant family, carrying the
burden of high expectations all her life, and facing constant,
near-daily scrutiny and bigotry. It became clear that her rigid
exterior was a protective shell that had served a purpose
while also keeping her from connecting with her own humanity and the experiences of people around her.

I could see different well-intentioned, misinformed protectors (WIMPs)—most prominently the perfectionist and the
imposter—show up in her words and demeanor. She felt like

she had lost her sense of self by putting on the armor that seemed necessary at one point but now had become restrictive and limiting in her role leading a large legal team. After she finished her courageous share, I observed, "We wake up most days trying to be someone we already are." The entire room breathed a collective sigh of relief.

Too often, we try to make ourselves into leaders who accept certain parts of our humanity and uniqueness while hiding, burying, or denying other parts, such as fear, insecurity, and doubt, we deem unworthy of someone in a leadership position. In that workshop, I reminded the participants that we can also start from the other side, knowing that we already are who we've always been. We are not lost, just buried underneath a bunch of corporate BS, personal failures, and outdated coping mechanisms.

In that room, we gave each other permission to be fully human and allowed our leadership capabilities to grow out of that acceptance. I needed to hear what I told Mehrsa and all the other participants. Working in this field, it is not lost on me that what I teach is what I still need to learn myself again and again.

YOU CAN'T DISCONNECT HUMAN SUFFERING FROM YOUR WORK PERSONA

We sometimes believe that being human gets in the way of being an effective leader and that self-compassion will make us weaker and less decisive, competitive, and respectable. I had spent over fifteen years of my career in professional talent development when my exposure to the concept of self-compassion illuminated the fact that I was not the best

FIGURE 8. The Backward/Forward Duality. How do we harness our common humanity to accept our past by looking backward so we can gain clarity on how to move forward?

leader I could be. I was successful in helping thousands of clients become better leaders, yet I felt like a hypocrite. For a long time, I was too caught up in my identity as a leadership coach and couldn't accept the parts of me that stood in contradiction to the concepts I taught to others.

I felt like I was sliding deeper and deeper into an identity crisis. I was an expert in leadership development, yet I questioned the very idea of what it meant to be a leader. I witnessed people transform their lives, communicate and lead more effectively, and rewire self-limiting beliefs. I finally figured out why I could help others become better leaders while feeling unfulfilled myself. I was so focused on changing others that I mistook their growth for my own. I confused their courage to take a hard look at themselves for my own bravery. I immersed myself in their development so completely that I neglected to advance my own progress.

I recognized that the false narratives my coaching clients and workshop participants revealed to me were the same ones playing in my own head on endless repeat. *You're not good enough. You're a fraud. You'll never make it. Don't show weakness.* Though I was a witness to their courageous

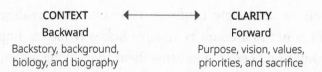

FIGURE 9. Gaining Balance between Context and Clarity. The duality of context/clarity corresponds to the backward/forward on-ramps for the Ward Model and represents acceptance.

transformation, I'd completely eliminated myself from the equation.

I pretended to be the sage on the stage while being lost in my WIMP's self-protection. My two jobs were being a leadership coach and, at the same time, hiding that I wasn't a great leader myself. I maintained an emotional distance to protect myself not only from the pain of others but also, perhaps more importantly, from my own pain. I wasn't honest or open to the profound growth I preached to the thousands of leaders in my programs.

The duality of backward and forward illustrates how understanding our shared humanity can help us accept what we've done to get us here so we can gain clarity on how to move forward (figures 8 and 9).

LOOKING BACKWARD TO MOVE FORWARD

The false stories we create and WIMPs we ascribe to are not necessarily based on facts but constructed based on personal history, cultural background, biological processes, and societal constraints. We can't change the fact that our brains are wired to prefer biased information that matches long-held beliefs or seemingly confirms aspiration over reality. The point is not to attempt to remove biases (which is impossible) but to get better at noticing them, identifying where they come from, and knowing what to do with them. Recognizing that all of these layers inform your perspective can help you hold your opinions, thoughts, and stories more loosely, inviting curiosity, flexibility, and nuance.

This is easier said than done in leadership situations, where people depend on us and we are required to make quick decisions that we believe had better be correct or else we will be seen as ineffective or bad leaders. When we carry the heavy burden of responsibility and of needing to have the right answer to every problem, our brains are easily triggered to activate automatic thought responses. These responses are often riddled with biases and false narratives that lead to fear-based decision-making. However, if we leverage self-compassion to cultivate a mindset of flexibility rather than rigidity and learn to cherish the times we're proven wrong, our mind and leadership ability expand.

Of course, biases and false narratives aren't the only ways our brains trip us up. Whether or not we're consciously aware of it, our personal pain will significantly impact our professional lives and leadership performance. You may never find yourself in a rock-bottom moment before realizing that a lack of self-compassion for your humanity has been bleeding into your performance at work. Instead, you may feel a consistent tension, edginess, or frustration—a vague sense that something isn't right. Accepting that these difficult situations and feelings are part of being human is the only way to deal with them in a productive way.

EXERCISE » How Self-Compassion Can Keep You from Getting Stuck in Suffering

We suffer because we're human. If suffering is too strong a word for you, call it stress, burnout, adversity, pain, or discomfort. Whether you got passed over for the promotion, have to lay off your team, or be accountable to the board for not meeting benchmarks, self-compassion offers an effective way to deal with intense emotions and moments of suffering. When a difficult situation arises, I use this three-part mantra Kristin Neff calls a "self-compassion break"[47] to help me deal:

» **This is a moment of suffering.** This helps you tap into mindful awareness.

» **Suffering (or pain, stress, discomfort) is a part of life.** This helps you accept pain as part of being human.

» **May I be kind (or patient, gentle, forgiving) to myself?** This helps you be accountable for self-regulation by practicing self-kindness.

This is a moment of suffering.
Saying this in your head or out loud is a way to acknowledge that something difficult is going on and you're actively bringing it into your awareness. If "suffering" sounds too intense, use a variation, such as "I'm in pain right now," "This is very stressful," or "This situation is uncomfortable." Name the emotion you're feeling, such as anger, and be specific about why you're feeling angry.

» I'm angry that I wasn't heard at the meeting / feel undervalued at this company.

» I'm frustrated that I didn't get it right / experienced failure.

» I'm disappointed that I received a bad performance review / struggled to make the requested changes to my leadership style.

Pay attention to where the emotion surfaces in your body. Is it a constriction or tightness in your throat or chest? Is there a buzzing in your head? Do your fists clench? Take your palms and rub them together to create warmth, then place your hands on your throat or chest and imagine warmth and light streaming into that body part. Yes, it's weird. Just try it out (you can even roll your eyes the entire time you're doing it), and see what happens.

Acceptance of the emotion helps you avoid getting hijacked by it or trying to bottle it back up. This way, you can acknowledge and honor it without letting it overpower you, lashing out in anger, and acting impulsively. Tapping into the anger will feel strange at first, but it will allow you to get back in the driver's seat and act rather than react.

Suffering (or pain, stress, discomfort) is a part of life.
Saying this to yourself takes the shame out of the experience, allows you to accept your pain as an integral part of being human, and reminds you that other leaders you don't even know may be suffering at the same moment.

May I be kind (or patient, gentle, forgiving) to myself?
Sometimes you may feel like doing an actual act of service and caring for yourself, like getting a drink of water, taking a nap, or asking for a hug. At work, you may take a quick walk, call a friend for a pep talk, or get some lunch. Sometimes you

may just offer yourself patience or forgiveness, depending on what you need right then. All of these options show that you're taking accountability for meeting your own needs.

Being mindfully aware of your own suffering and accepting the shared human experience of pain allows you to take accountability for regulating strong emotions and soothing yourself so you can continue moving forward rather than getting stuck.

WHY THIS EXERCISE WILL MAKE YOU STRONGER, NOT WEAKER

David Goggins, former Navy SEAL and current endurance athlete and author of *Can't Hurt Me*, believes accepting pain and suffering is important in achieving growth and success.[48] While this book may seem contrary to Goggins's approach, we both agree that suffering is a natural part of life to embrace rather than avoid. Goggins's modern-day stoicism is very much aligned with the practice of self-compassion to alleviate suffering. Self-compassionate leadership isn't a way to avoid pain—instead, it strengthens us to face the inevitable storms rather than cowering in fear. Suffering helps us push through the pain and build resilience so we can overcome future obstacles. It all starts with making a conscious decision to see suffering as an inevitable part of human life and, therefore, our work and careers.

I'm not advocating that you torture yourself by adding to your suffering, going it alone, or denying yourself rest. But, like Goggins, I know we often shortchange ourselves and get stuck in the "backward" stories of self-doubt and fear. We are much more capable than we think we are. Embracing suffering is one way to tap into our hidden potential and accomplish "forward" feats we never thought possible.

According to Goggins, taking ownership of our own suffering allows it to become a means of personal transformation. When we use self-compassion to take responsibility for the pain of our self-doubt, it turns into a catalyst for growth in all aspects of our lives, especially in our leadership practice. This is the opposite of the trite and overused "no regrets" mantra you see plastered all over social media.

"NO REGRETS" CAN UNDERMINE GROWTH

So often, we think that abiding by the mantra of "no regrets" shows how evolved we are. It proclaims to the world that everything we've done has become a learning opportunity and that we're consistently living our best lives and wildest dreams.

If that's genuinely true for someone, great. But often, when I sense an inability to self-reflect, I call bullshit. "No regrets" becomes the mechanism people use to stay above the other part of their human experience, which is "shit's hard." We suffer, make mistakes, and hurt others, even when we don't want to and try as much as possible to avoid it. We can't escape our humanity. "No regrets" is often nothing more than a feeble attempt to refuse accepting the parts of our humanity that are uncomfortable and painful.

At the other extreme are those who are stuck in the past, mired in shame and self-loathing over things they said or did years or decades ago. When our perfectionist WIMP runs the show, we can't forgive ourselves when we fall short. We can't leave the past where it belongs; instead, we allow it to become a projection of what our future will inevitably look like. That pattern creates a lot of anxiety and fear, of course. We never get to the other side of regret, where there's a lesson waiting for us, a recalibration, a deeper understanding, a liberation from incessant guilt, and the motivation to begin again.

WOO-WOO WINS 》 Mike

Mike Buccilia found himself overwhelmed in his new executive marketing position at a start-up founded by friends. He's the kind of outgoing, charismatic guy who's genuinely interested in people, an excellent conversationalist, and fun to be around. He came into the role with the confidence that he would excel, just as he had throughout his illustrious career in sales and marketing. As a top performer in his field, he was used to exceeding everyone's expectations, but now he was stuck, unable to make simple decisions. He felt the stakes were higher than ever, and the chaotic, high-pressure start-up environment soon activated his fight/flight/freeze/fawn response. And we all know who shows up in this volatile stage—WIMPs!

Everything felt like life or death, although logically Mike knew it wasn't. Instead of rising to the occasion as usual, Mike found himself collapsing under the pressure. The imposter WIMP added massive anxiety, making Mike worry about whether he was really cut out for the position and terrified that the executive team felt the same way. Every mistake he made weighed heavily on his mind and kept him ruminating for days, even weeks. His perfectionist WIMP got stuck obsessing over his past errors, creating further doubt that he was capable of facing the next looming challenge.

Mike recalls that self-forgiveness was one of the most valuable practices he came across in his quest to find relief from his past regrets and future anxieties: "It wasn't even something I knew I could do for myself." This was a dramatic shift. It marked the dawning of the realization that more of the same—piling on the self-criticism—was not the solution: "I had no idea how much the inner critic, the judge, was driving my behaviors, and I didn't believe there was any other way. That is what made me 'successful'—it worked, until it failed completely." There are many definitions of forgiveness, but a major component is acceptance of a situation as it is, not as we wish it were.

Discovering the practice of self-compassion opened up a whole new world for Mike. He realized he didn't need any external validation or achievements to validate his worth. It may seem like this realization could dampen motivation, but it actually opens up true confidence and makes carrying the same load feel lighter and less intense. Mike learned that he already knew how to do the job. He recommitted to looking backward not to beat himself up but to use past mistakes as learning experiences to shape a better future and move forward confidently. "I learned there was another way beyond simply looking for external validation to prove my worth," Mike explained to me. "I had the resources within me to feel validated and worthy of my role and work. We can care for, nurture, and grow ourselves."

As he practiced forgiving himself, he found it easier to forgive others instead of holding grudges for small slights. Mike strengthened his capacity for empathy and relating to others in an open and authentic way, acknowledging and understanding their struggles as well as his own.

This shift not only helped Mike start to enjoy the learning and growth provided by a start-up roller coaster but also opened up new possibilities for him. After the start-up was successfully acquired, Mike was able to take time off to focus on more self-kindness, rest, and move on to start several new business ventures of his own.

I need to warn you that self-forgiveness can trigger a lot of resistance and dismissal. *It's just too uncomfortable for me, sorry.* Ask yourself what exactly you don't like about self-forgiveness? Do you see it as shirking responsibility or falsely atoning for your mistakes? Do you find false comfort in thinking that as long as you punish yourself, you don't need to be forgiven? If you're struggling with the concept, think of it as acceptance of what is—the reality of the situation, including your involvement or contribution.

EXERCISE » How to Practice Self-Forgiveness

Take a Ceremonial Forgiveness Walk

» Grab a stack of index cards or Post-it notes, and write one thing you want to forgive yourself for on each card.

» Choose a peaceful spot, preferably in nature, to go for a ceremonial walk.

» As you take each step, read one card out loud. Repeat this process until you feel complete. You may experience a lightness as the burden of personal resentment lifts. Remember that forgiving ourselves does not mean we have to forget what we did or, more important, the lessons we learned.

» At the end of the walk, tear up or burn the cards. This step in the ceremony helps to transform the backward story into a new forward narrative of personal accountability, growth, and self-acceptance.

Admittedly, this ceremony can feel a bit esoteric, but it symbolizes letting go of instances that have burned inside of you for too long. You accept that these things happened. You no longer have to carry the shame. If this this option feels too fringe, try this instead:

Write a Letter of Forgiveness

» Write a letter from yourself to yourself, forgiving all the incidents you would have written on those index cards.

» If that's still too uncomfortable, pretend you're writing a note to a good friend. You're still telling that "friend" what you need to hear yourself, but it can remove some of the initial awkwardness.

» Feel free to burn or tear up the letter or note when you're done. Ultimately, this exercise is for your eyes only.

Self-compassion allows us to see regret as the beautiful and painful human experience it is. Equanimity—mental calmness and composure in difficult situations—allows us to embrace both sides of our humanity, the ups and downs, without dismissing, ignoring, or bottling up the experiences that have caused us or others significant pain. There is, indeed, a lesson in every "backward" regret, but we can't gloss over or rush through that learning process. Self-compassion offers equanimity to help us process regret without spiraling into self-hate, shame, denial, or hyperpositivity. When we look backward to reflect on and learn from our regrets, they can become powerful signposts pointing forward to shape our values and vision. Self-compassion contextualizes our past experiences and helps us gain clarity for the future.

When I look back at my life, my worst regrets often center on situations in which I didn't trust myself. I believed the opinions others had of me and the false stories I told myself. These deep regrets have become the fuel and motivation to live a life more aligned with my values and priorities. Self-compassion has taught me those rock-bottom moments of pain I've suffered or caused others are scary caves to venture into, but they hold a stunning treasure. It is often the most painful regrets that have brought the most profound self-awareness and wisdom, once I allowed the pain to break me open.

The regret over trying to fit into corporate culture for decades finally prompted me to start my own leadership development and coaching consultancy. The regret I feel about hurting people I cared about in personal and professional relationships allowed me to work on myself and make positive changes. My own struggles with applying self-compassion spurred me to write this book to share my experience. Through it all, self-compassion helped me keep the shame at bay, so I could face this important internal work.

It's this internal work looking backward that led me to clarify my purpose, values, and needs going forward.

YOUR PURPOSE AND VALUES PROPEL YOU FORWARD

According to the 2022 Gallup *State of the Global Workplace* report, more than half of Americans (57 percent) report disengaging at work and sleepwalking through their days without passion or energy, because they don't find value and meaning in their tasks. "When employees are engaged and thriving, they experience significantly less stress, anger, and health problems. Nevertheless, globally, only 9% of employees are in that thriving and engaged category," according to the report.[49]

While companies spent lots of time in the 1990s and early 2000s talking about work-life balance and adding foosball tables and free snacks to offices, there is now a growing desire for depth and purpose. Employers are concerned with engagement and satisfaction in the current reality of working 24/7 with global teams scattered throughout different time zones. An increasingly remote workforce and a global pandemic have both helped galvanize demand for a new sense of meaning that permeates and merges our personal and professional lives. People are no longer satisfied living on autopilot, following outdated corporate playbooks and narrow societal templates.

The Gallup report also notes that a staggering 89 percent of professionals feel they're suffering from burnout and 81 percent say it's worse now than before the pandemic. This tells me that the pandemic didn't create our longing for meaningful work but that the number of people thinking and talking about it has finally reached critical mass. In a world full of uncertainty, many of us no longer want to be stuck in jobs and relationships that make us unhappy, live in communities that don't accept us, or live our lives according to someone else's wishes. The pandemic disrupted our normal work routines and gave us the opportunity to rethink what it means to have a fulfilling, successful, happy, and meaningful life.

VALUES AS A BY-PRODUCT OF YOUR FAMILY AND CULTURE

This collective reckoning on whether our work has real meaning and connects to what matters most to us is exciting. And very, very confusing.

Few of us are naturally great at figuring out what truly matters to us so we can live, work, and lead in accordance with our core values. We know our favorite places to travel, the food we like to eat, and what we love doing in our free time, but many of us are figuring out for the first time who we truly are as individuals. Even if we think we know what drives and motivates us, we can fall into the trap of making these assumptions about ourselves without really knowing where they came from or questioning their validity. Upon closer examination of our values, we realize it's what our parents taught us, what our peer group deems acceptable, or what our WIMPs tell us.

Definitions of success and conceptions of what leaders look like are often prescribed by our family, our culture, and the organizations we work in. When we think of Ivy League academia, Bay Area start-ups, or multinational legacy corporations, we likely imagine a distinct set of values guiding these organizations and a particular type of leader at the head. We rarely question whether these organizational values align with our personal values. And just as important: Are these personal values our own, or have we unquestioningly adopted them from our parents, teachers, peers, religious leaders, politicians, or bosses?

Adopting Values to Fit In

We are biologically conditioned to change who we are in an attempt to fit in and be accepted by our manager, leadership, peer group, family system, social network, or workplace. While this can calm our brain and keep us from experiencing the urge to launch into a fight/flight/freeze/fawn response, changing who we are to fit in can also have negative consequences.

In my case, I knew from an early age that I wanted to be an entrepreneur, but entrepreneurship is a terrifying endeavor without solid guardrails or clear required credentials or expertise. I didn't know where to start, so I buried that dream. I found myself working in corporate America, feeling like a misfit much of the time because I wasn't honoring my truth. I never subscribed to the political games, unnecessary meetings, and inefficient hierarchy. I hated that my future progress was largely in the hands of one person, my manager. Instead of exploring why I felt out of place, I tried to conform. For years, I went against the grain of who I am: I wasn't going with the current of my life; I was fighting against it. Now, with a few years of distance from that period of my life and experience running my own business, it's clear that I'm certifiably unemployable. Entrepreneurship isn't right for everyone, but it gave me the creative and operational freedom I craved so desperately while working for other people.

My biggest regrets are those times in my life when I didn't trust my own gut to do what was right for me. I dismissed my internal warning signs that I was out of alignment, or did what I thought others expected of me, even though I knew the job or the relationship wasn't right for me. Admittedly, fear kept me from recognizing the warning signs. When I was at a low point in my life and career, it took experiencing that full-blown panic attack on my living-room floor for me to realize I needed a fundamental change. The red flags had been there from the beginning, but I chose not to pay attention. My life and work had been completely out of alignment with my values, and I was paying the price.

Clarifying Your Unique Purpose, Needs, and Values As a Leader

Stepping out of autopilot and consciously exerting curiosity to revel in deep self-reflection is not habitual for most of us. It feels awkward, uncomfortable, and even silly. We simply don't know how to do it in practice. Self-reflection, actively thinking about our own feelings and behaviors and the reasons that might lie beneath them, is not a value we hold in US culture. We frequently chase the next goal and status symbol rather than slowing down and looking inside to ask ourselves if that's what's truly important to us. We are not used to this level of honesty and stillness.

As the Buddhist psychologist Jon Kabat-Zinn says in his book *Wherever You Go, There You Are*, "If we hope to go any-where or develop ourselves in any way, we can only step from where we are standing. If we don't really know where we are standing . . . we may only go in circles."[50] Through stillness, we find where we are.

We may find aspects of ourselves we don't like, discover dreams and desires that stand in opposition to our current life, or realize our core values don't align with those of the people around us. Most terrifyingly, we may recognize that we do know what we want or need, which will require us to accept the truth that maybe we're not on the right path or we're missing out on true fulfillment on our current path. Perhaps we put in decades as a leader in a particular field that's not the right fit, spent years working on a relationship that's ultimately beyond repair, or held onto a set of beliefs and behaviors that once served us only to learn they're now holding us back. Change can be scary, and slowing down enough to see that we've been heading in the wrong direction for years or decades is often enough to send us back into autopilot.

Autonomy is one of my core values that hasn't changed over the decades, but the way I live it has evolved based on my age, experience, circumstances, needs, and wants. In my twenties, autonomy meant spending time with my friends whenever and however I pleased. Now that I'm not on my own anymore and have responsibilities to my family, autonomy means creating the life I want on my own terms and leaving a legacy I'm proud of. I choose the clients I work with and the meetings I take. I have full creative control over my work and what I put out into the world.

The key to self-reflection that brings deep awareness around our values is to do it regularly, honestly, and with compassion. Self-reflection requires self-compassion to counteract the self-judgment likely to creep up in this process. Instead of focusing on making ourselves fit into preexisting molds of societal and familial expectations, we need to look out and up to imagine all that's possible for us outside the box. What do I want most in my life? What does success look like? Along with difficulty and discomfort, self-reflection also brings clarity, calm, quiet joy, and a sense of direction and purpose.

In short, accepting your current reality while deploying self-compassion is the most underrated process to getting the life you want.

EXERCISE » Uncover Your Values

This is a free writing exercise to help you uncover your values. To get the most out of the exercise, be as honest as possible. This means you may experience some discomfort. You may find out some surprising truths that feel disorienting at first. When answering questions like this, it's very easy to confuse what's true for us with what we think our answer should be. We may start listing socially acceptable answers or values we believe to be important to others whose opinions we respect. Long ago I set up an online dating profile that said I loved traveling (I hadn't left the country in years) and hiking (I went on a single hike that summer). It was at best aspirational and at worst inauthentic. Either way, it's helpful to ask why.

Start by writing down your top five values.
Examples: autonomy, creativity, generosity, kindness, honesty, joy, peace, clarity, family, friendship, excellence, abundance.

If you're challenged to find five clear winners, consider these questions:

» Recall a peak experience in your life. What values do you associate with this experience?

» What are your biggest pet peeves? What do these frustrations reveal about your values?

» What makes you angry? What was the topic of your last argument or debate? Which of your values was violated?

» What brings you joy or admiration from other people? Does this hint at a value that feels easy to uphold?

» Imagine you have five years to live. What do you change about your life, and what does it say about your values?

Answer as honestly as possible, withholding judgment from yourself, and with the understanding that nobody else needs to see your responses.

Then, repeat the following steps for all your top five values.

» Name your top value. *We'll use my value of autonomy as an example.*

» What does *autonomy* mean to you in your personal and professional life? What is your definition of this value? How is your definition different or the same as other definitions?

» Is this a fixed or changing value (has *autonomy* always been important to you, or did a specific incident or event help you realize its importance)? Have you expressed this value differently during various life stages, contexts, or relationships? Why?

» Does your personal and professional life align with *autonomy*? Why or why not? What is one thing you could do to become more aligned?

» Did any of your answers surprise you? Did you relearn something about yourself that you had forgotten? Once we get honest about our values, the next step is to act on what we say is important to us and take a closer look at how much time and effort we invest in living in alignment with those values.

Our emotions are excellent data points for uncovering deeper knowledge about ourselves and our values. Pleasant feelings like joy, excitement, or enthusiasm can become emotional cues to ask yourself which of your values are being highlighted or elevated in that moment. The same goes for feelings we often experience as more difficult, such as anger, frustration, or sadness, because they can show us that we might be out of alignment with our values. *I'm angry because the meeting ran long, and we didn't get to the part of the presentation I prepared.* This emotional data point can illustrate your values of diligence, respect for your own and other people's efforts, and time management.

Only by understanding the forces and motivations behind your thoughts, feelings, and actions will you know how you got to where you are today, where you want to go next, and how you will get there.

Finding (or Creating) Communities with Aligned Values

Once we have done the challenging work to clarify our personal purpose, needs, and values, we've gained important self-awareness and acceptance of our current reality. Channeling this self-awareness and acceptance into action can be even more difficult. It takes courage to live our values regardless of social, professional, and cultural backlash.

My past regrets give context to who I am today and how I got here. They're also a powerful reminder that to be happy and successful, I need to be curious about the world around me and within me and then courageous enough to act on what I discover. The decisions we've already made do not dictate our future choices, but they can offer important lessons and rich data points to inform our next steps. There are opportunities to make different choices at each reflection point. Knowing my values gives me guideposts to check in with myself. *Is my life aligned with my internal values?* There is a power in trusting myself even when it goes against the status quo or others' ideas about what I should do.

In his book *Transitions,* William Bridges explains that the neutral zone is the space between endings and new beginnings.[51] I ask myself: *How can I learn from this past challenge without letting it define me and forgive myself so I can create a different future?* The duality of backward and forward, context and clarity, helps me to mindfully unpack my baggage before intentionally repacking only the items that would best serve me in my new beginning (figure 10).

Knowing who we truly are and what we value most is a

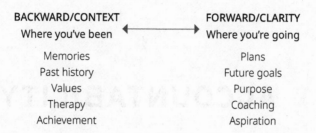

FIGURE 10. Backward/Context and Forward/Clarity. The tension of backward/context and forward/clarity can look like this in practice.

central part of our individual and shared humanity that we must leverage to find or create the communities and situations that will allow us to thrive. Self-awareness and acceptance of our current reality are essential for designing the life we want, becoming the leader we were meant to be, and living according to our highest values. How? By taking accountability.

6 » ACCOUNTABILITY

Finding Comfort and Courage

A ship in the harbor is safe, but that's not what ships
are built for.

JOHN A. SHEDD, *Salt from My Attic*

Jess Almlie is an executive adviser and powerhouse strategist
in learning and development whose intelligence commands
your attention. It takes effort to keep up with her work ethic
and tireless curiosity. As the oldest of ten children, Jess had always felt a tremendous responsibility to be strong, to achieve,
and to be the very best personally and professionally. What
her well-intentioned, misinformed protector (WIMP) had
been telling her for years was that she wasn't allowed to make
mistakes because other people would suffer as a result of her
incompetence. She was the designated rescuer and fixer until
one day she got so sick that she couldn't fix herself. She tried
to do what she'd always done—listen to her perfectionist
drill-sergeant WIMP and push through—but things got so bad

that she couldn't get out of bed. Her entire body was hurting. She was in so much pain, yet her suffering was invisible to everyone.

"I only went to the doctor because I could no longer function at my job. I was diagnosed with Hashimoto's thyroiditis, an autoimmune disease that causes the underfunctioning of my thyroid. My body was attacking itself just like I'd been attacking myself mentally all along. And yet, in the beginning, I tried to beat my body into submission, criticizing every move I'd made that day. Why was I still so exhausted? Why couldn't I fix myself? Did I forget to take my supplements? Was there gluten in my lunch? Did I not sleep enough? It was always my fault that I felt miserable.

"My well-intentioned, misinformed protector (WIMP) looks like this bright pink wheel that's constantly whirring and making this high-pitched buzzing sound. It's a spinning, fuzzy whirl of all my anxiety and worry and merciless self-criticism. I try to ignore it. I bury it in work. I just keep pushing it away. I'm scared to take a moment to pause and really look at it and acknowledge its presence. Because if it stops spinning, I'm afraid it will just melt into a puddle of pink goo representing a deep sadness."

Our WIMPs directly impact where we fall on the spectrum between leeward comfort and windward courage. Does your WIMP tell you that you'll fail anyway, so why even try? You might rarely push yourself to your limit and stay in the safe harbor, never venturing out. Is your WIMP of the hard-ass variety, berating you for being weak and never good enough? You might overcompensate by white-knuckling your entire

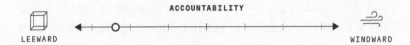

ACCOUNTABILITY

LEEWARD   WINDWARD

FIGURE 11. The Leeward/Windward Duality. How do we take accountability to balance our leeward need for comfort with our windward sense of courage?

life, never taking a break to catch your breath and eventually burning out.

Our WIMPs play the role of villain in this epic battle for power in our brains. An internal monologue about being bad, stupid, lazy, weak, selfish, or incapable is familiar to most of us, although the flavor and tone may vary depending on our specific WIMPs. Especially when it comes to practicing self-compassion to counter the not-good-enough narrative, our perfectionist or achiever WIMPs can plunge into over-drive, telling us we're weak, soft, or making excuses.

The tension between courage and comfort offers us an op-portunity to foster psychological safety within ourselves so we can face our fears. Sometimes we need to lean into the wind, and sometimes we need to seek shelter (figures 11 and 12). Self-kindness, especially as a leader, can help you hold yourself accountable with kindness and respect. Hitting rock bottom—our most painful failures—can become a source of self-awareness and a chance to practice self-kindness, as can our seemingly insignificant pet peeves. Self-kindness allows us to use humor to soften the blows we're dealt and under-stand that a blunder is not a career-ending mistake.

COURAGE	COMFORT
Windward	Leeward
Setting boundaries, getting outside our comfort zone, making sacrifices for our goals, and establishing new habits	Shelter from the wind, humanizing our mistakes, deploying humor and self-kindness

FIGURE 12. Gaining Balance between Courage and Comfort. The duality of courage/comfort corresponds to the windward/leeward on-ramps for the Ward Model and represents accountability.

YOUR INNER WIMP IS A JERK WITH GOOD INTENTIONS

Our WIMPs are here to stay. Since we don't have the ability to evict our WIMPs and go "no contact," we must accept that it will be a lifelong relationship to manage. Why? Our WIMPs are a built-in survival mechanism, trying to keep us safe. *Don't speak up, because you could be embarrassed. Don't make a fool of yourself, play it safe—you need this job! Don't dream too big, because you may not get what you want. Don't have that vulnerable conversation, because you could get rejected.*

In some situations—say, if you aren't in a safe, supportive environment—your WIMPs might actually protect you from harm. Your people-pleaser WIMP may keep you from speaking up in a meeting or taking on a high-visibility project when the risks of dismissal or ridicule outweigh the rewards. You may avoid sharing your self-judgment or doubt with your manager, fearing that, based on their leadership style, they may perceive you as weak.

However, we're fully grown adults with the ability to manage difficult challenges, so we can actively choose whether we want to listen to our WIMPs or not. We can recognize when it's smart to play it safe, and when it's worth going out of our comfort zone.

YOUR INNER WIMP: THE ROOMMATE YOU CAN'T EVICT

Although living with one or multiple WIMPs that never shut up and sometimes fight with each other can feel like living with annoying roommates you can't evict, you *can* set boundaries. You may have noticed that the more you ignore your WIMP, the pushier it becomes. Your WIMP might not be a certified hard-ass berating you all day, but even the seemingly more helpful iterations of this unwelcome roomie, such as the achiever, people pleaser, or imposter, can wreak havoc, which is all the worse if their words are couched in concern. Because they're so well intentioned, we may not be able to recognize them for what they are, especially if they're not overtly cruel and critical.

Maybe your WIMP is like a well-meaning parent, an older brother, or a mentor who has good intentions but wants to tell you what to do rather than encouraging you to find your own way. They knew you back when and are unwilling to update their opinion of you based on your growth and change. They keep wanting to put you back in a box, reattach the labels they're comfortable with, and reconfirm outdated narratives about you instead of accepting new information.

WOO-WOO WINS » Jess

Jess had attended one of my workshops and started using one of the self-compassion practices I'd taught the attendees. It's a simple body scan check-in, where you pause and assess any physical sensations, feelings, and thoughts. Then you name what is happening without judgment. *My throat is tight. I feel dread about this presentation. I should have prepared better.* Then you focus on a small kindness you can give to yourself. For Jess, this was the key to getting the pink whirl of anxiety to stop spinning. She was no longer afraid of looking at the melty goo at the core of herself and asking what she needed.

"Instead of focusing on fixing, I practiced loving myself, all of me, including the pink spinny thing and all the parts I'd always been ashamed of or tried to hide—including my Hashimoto's thyroiditis. I realized you can't heal a body you hate. I started journaling and working with my well-intentioned, misinformed protector (WIMP). I listened to my needs. Sometimes I wanted to be loved and needed physical affection. Sometimes I desired to be thanked and appreciated. Sometimes I needed to be heard. I decided to love the pink fuzzy knots exactly as they were. In a way, I became grateful for my illness, because it made me aware of my cruel WIMP and helped me learn how to truly love myself."

YOUR WELL-INTENTIONED, MISINFORMED PROTECTOR IS PART OF YOU

Besides understanding that our WIMPs often come from a place of misguided protection, we must understand, just like Jess did, that we are not separate from our WIMPs. They're part of us. There is no us versus them. We can think of our WIMPs less as separate entities and more as the parts of us that act out of fear or resistance to change, wanting to protect us and keep us safe, sometimes using cruel words and methods to do so. The more we push back against this voice that represents an essential part of us, the more we'll be locked into a struggle against ourselves.

Instead of trying to dominate your WIMP, accept it as a part of you that serves a limited purpose but that you have no obligation to follow. Self-compassion can help you accept the scared, defensive, judgmental, and cruel part of you and gently choose a different path. As Iona Holloway, author and founder of Brave Thing, explains, "Freedom does not exist until you can hold the worst parts of you gently."[52] Rather than battling your WIMPs, accept the thoughts as they are, knowing you have the freedom to make a different choice, reframe an old story, and go another way.

I sometimes quietly talk to my WIMPs. I thank them for trying to protect me but firmly state that I trust myself in this situation. Instead of a "fuck off" approach, try "thanks, but I got it." The effort you waste fighting with your WIMP is better spent practicing self-compassion, vulnerability, and courage to recommit to your purpose and make choices aligned with your values, regardless of what your WIMP wants to talk you into.

EXERCISE » Nobody Is Coming to Save You— Taking Accountability for Your Life

Instead of defaulting to our WIMPs in pursuit of leadership development and excellence, we are likely to find the combination of self-kindness, curiosity, and honesty to be more successful in generating the self-awareness and acceptance that allow us to take accountability and follow our values. Accountability represents the first step in putting our red arrow on the map indicating where we are, before we can make any decisions about where to go.

There are lots of ways to assess how you spend your time, energy, and money to make sure it lines up with your overall vision for life. This accountability exercise will help you reflect on whether the forces that drive your life decisions are your core values and will give you an opportunity to calibrate your actions to bring them into alignment with those values.

This exercise is for your eyes only, so be honest with yourself. Begin by recalling the five core values you identified in chapter 5, and keep them in mind while you write your answers to the following questions by hand, type them into your phone, or dictate them into a voice app:

1. What is your personal definition of success?

2. What strengths or values do you appreciate most in others? Are they the same or complementary to your values? Can you bring more people with these values into your life?

3. What puts you in a flow state (such as being highly engaged in a challenging project that makes you lose your sense of time)?

4. When did you last push yourself out of your comfort zone, and how did it feel?

5. Who are the most important social connections in your life, and do they match the kind of relationships you long for?

6. Talking to yourself as your own best friend, what would you recommend as your best next step (more rest, a new hobby, a different exercise routine, a career or relationship change)?

Self-awareness can lead to two extreme responses: burying your head in the sand and going back to autopilot, or turning your life upside down and doing a full 180. Deploy self-kindness to slow down, pace yourself, make decisions deliberately, and take action consciously. Just as it works better to approach your WIMP gently, aligning your life more with your values rather than your WIMP's ideas must be done patiently and kindly to be sustainable. You can't do this overnight or in a morning's commute to work.

WOO-WOO WINS » Dan

My client Dan had a strong fixer / doer / problem-solver mindset. He always felt the need to be right in conversations and prove his intellectual horsepower. If you're thinking of a hard-ass WIMP with a touch of achiever, you're right on. I introduced Dan to the practice of journaling so he could try out self-kindness in private first. I instructed him to write about his frustrations with big projects and colleagues, his needs and feelings, perceived threats and weaknesses, and the facts of the situation versus the assumptions, interpretations, and stories that automatically came up for him.

When supplier issues threatened an important product launch he was leading, Dan was upset to the point where he couldn't sleep at night. He was stuck ruminating over the situation and worried about his future with the company if the launch was delayed. At 2:00 a.m. one night, he pulled out the journal and wrote until his mind was empty. He emailed me the next day to tell me he slept like a baby and woke up feeling refreshed and ready to tackle the day. If you want to try this exercise for yourself, set a timer for fifteen minutes and write whatever comes to your mind without stopping, re-reading, or editing yourself in the process. The quality of your writing doesn't matter. Don't judge your grammar or spelling. Treat this as a brain dump to send the thoughts spinning inside your head out and onto the paper. Pay attention to how you feel afterward.

Dan's openness to experiment with self-kindness, even though he'd been doing the opposite for much of his career, allowed him to see the objective value in it, even when it felt uncomfortable to practice.

Self-kindness can help us accept that we all suffer and struggle, without creating further pain for ourselves on top of the existing challenge. In her article "How to Love Yourself for Real," therapist Amanda McCracken explains Buddhist teaching about suffering as a tale of two arrows.[53] The first arrow we're shot with is an unfortunate event that happens outside of our direct control, such as Dan's supplier issues. Whether you contract a life-altering illness, are unexpectedly laid off, or get hurt in a car accident, these are all first arrows that pierce your life in some unforeseen or dramatic way. Almost worse than the original arrows are the second ones we often shoot ourselves with after the fact. These are the stories we tell ourselves about the original suffering. *You're not good enough to keep your job. If you'd taken better care of yourself, you wouldn't be sick. If you weren't rushing this morning, you wouldn't have gotten into that accident.*

Dan practiced self-kindness by putting this philosophy into practice. Instead of listening to his WIMP saying *You suck, you should've known better. You really couldn't have fucked this situation up any worse,* he decided to accept that the situation itself sucked, without internalizing it to the point of self-flagellation. He started treating himself with the same kindness he would extend to a close friend who'd just gone through a similar situation. One of the most powerful practices Dan started was listing three things he appreciated about himself and three things he was grateful for in his life every night before going to sleep. This helped to rewire his mind to look for the good instead of magnifying and catastrophizing the bad.

SELF-KINDNESS IS NOT A LUXURY BUT A NECESSITY FOR ACCOUNTABILITY

Self-kindness means setting healthy boundaries, making time for yourself, resting, and reserving energy for activities that light you up because they're aligned with your values and passions. Self-kindness is not a luxury, but a necessity. Particularly in light of the immense responsibility you have as a leader, taking care of yourself benefits everyone around you.

Self-kindness is valuable on its own, but especially in the context of leadership, because it allows you to properly model how to set priorities and boundaries for your team. Shame paralyzes, but self-compassion activates. There is a significant difference between saying to yourself *I suck as a person* and *This situation sucks and I can do something about it.* The first is demoralizing and disempowering, while the second removes us from the problem just enough to become the author and creator of a potential solution. It's much harder to figure out what to do next if you judge yourself as an overall failure rather than dealing with a problem you can act upon.

Dealing with painful challenges is hard enough without piling on top of ourselves with all the most shameful stories we can conjure up. Self-kindness helps us accept the reality and inevitability of pain and suffering without creating more of it. This isn't to say that we never have any control over what happens to us. It may very well be that you got into a car accident because you weren't paying attention; that does make you partially responsible. However, most situations have so many contributing factors that it's easy to pick the most incriminating one and run with it, shaming ourselves with extreme criticism in the process.

Maybe you weren't paying attention because you're a single dad who was up with a sick kid all night, but you still had to go to work in the morning since you're the sole provider. When you contextualize your behavior, the facts often fall into place differently. You're not a bad, irresponsible father and person. You're a tired dad who had a momentary lapse. Rather than running with the most cruel narrative possible, self-kindness opens up a space for grace and the ability to look at the facts of a situation as if we're talking to a loved one.

SELF-KINDNESS ISN'T A COP-OUT: IT MAKES YOU A BETTER PERSON

The magic of self-kindness is twofold: it helps us extend kindness to ourselves rather than brutal judgment in painful situations, and it also encourages us to hold ourselves to a high ethical standard and take accountability. In this way, self-kindness allows us to manage the tension between leeward and windward, comforting ourselves while courageously facing what needs to change.

In 2016, researchers asked students to either complete an annoying task themselves or pawn it off on someone else.[54] Those who chose to pawn the task off to others were further divided into two subgroups. One did a self-compassion practice while the control group wrote about a random hobby. When the researchers asked participants how they felt about pawning off the annoying task to someone else, the students who'd completed the self-compassion practice took more responsibility for their actions and saw their selfish act as less acceptable than the control group. They held themselves to a higher moral standard. In short, self-kindness is good for us, the people around us, and society in general.

Too often, we hold onto a well-worn narrative and a vague contempt for self-compassion as weak, silly, soft, and needy. Nobody wants to be seen as needy in this culture of self-reliance, independence, and pulling ourselves up by our bootstraps. These myths about self-compassion keep us from accessing the connection, belonging, and fulfillment we so deeply crave and that drive us to achieve objectives bigger than ourselves and become someone others *want* to follow.

In fact, while writing this book, I've wondered how to talk about self-compassion without using the term itself. And I teach this stuff for a living! I feared that talking about the concept of self-compassion would turn off some of the people I most hope to reach with this book—people like me, who used to see self-compassion as an excuse, giving myself a pass, cutting myself too much slack, or shirking responsibility. Back then, I prided myself on doubling down and working harder, sometimes to the detriment of my physical and mental health. This only illustrates the depth of our discomfort with extending love, acceptance, and kindness to ourselves.

RESISTANCE FROM WITHIN AND WITHOUT

If you're still wincing at the concept of self-compassion, I get it. It takes time and effort to change. As you're applying the concepts in this book, remember that squirming at the idea of being kind to yourself is part of your conditioning rather than an indicator that it's actually cringe-worthy.

Understanding self-compassionate leadership while reading this book is one thing. Practicing it can bring on a whole different level of discomfort. You may feel challenged or defensive. You may experience self-criticism and judgment. Perhaps you'll ask yourself why you picked up this book in the first place now that it's time to put it into practice. *I don't need help with self-compassion. I just need to get on with my work, and I need my team to keep up.*

EXERCISE » **Work with Your Resistance**

If you find yourself wanting to pull back or shut down or close this book, take a step back and work with your resistance.

Look for physical, emotional, or mental signs of resistance, such as

» Physical: rolling your eyes, sighing, or shaking your head

» Emotional: feeling anxious, edgy, upset for no reason, frustrated, or angry

» Mental: hearing your WIMP telling you you're wasting your time or copping out, feeling judgmental or critical of yourself or others, or distracting yourself from the book's content

Once you've identified one or more signs of resistance, acknowledge them, set them aside, and consider the ideas you're reading about. Ask yourself these two questions:

» What does this sign of resistance have to teach me?

» What is my "yes/and" response?

  » EXAMPLE 1: *Yes*, I'm feeling angry with myself for letting things get so bad that I have to read about self-compassion, *and* I'm open to trying something new because what I've been doing isn't working.

  » EXAMPLE 2: *Yes*, I am judging others for giving me feedback about how my standards are too high when I think they just need to work harder, *and* there is a kernel of truth in that feedback, and I want to learn how to lead differently.

Doing this deep work takes effort, even when deploying self-compassion. Sometimes, self-compassion itself can trigger challenges, so it's essential to be prepared for these bumps in the road. Otherwise, these problems may start feeling like insurmountable issues that can lead you to resist the entire process.

SELF-COMPASSION CAN CAUSE BACKDRAFT

Backdraft is a firefighting term to describe what happens when you open a door or window to a hot or burning room that has been sealed off from airflow and thus has limited oxygen. When you open the door or window and introduce oxygen, the sudden influx of air will cause the flames inside to roar and burst out. Author Kristin Neff relates this concept to self-compassion, which provides us with an influx of self-discovery and awareness that can call forth not only beautiful emotions and thoughts, like love and kindness, but also difficult emotions, painful memories, and deep struggles.[55] We quickly realize that our bodies, hearts, and minds don't distinguish between "positive" and "negative" sensations, emotions, and thoughts in the way we've been conditioned. Once we open ourselves to feeling our feelings, we will experience more kindness and patience toward ourselves, along with long-held judgments and criticisms and pain we've bottled up for years or decades. In short, it may feel as if everything is coming out all at once, creating a potent swirl of emotions.

Once we start accepting ourselves, our WIMPs will make themselves known. Using self-compassion to accept the release of pent-up anger, sadness, grief, longing, and despair can

be overwhelming at first, because we're suddenly faced with
all that we've considered too ugly to look at. Everything we've
kept at bay, locked up, tried to avoid, and deny will eventually
rear its head and ask to be accepted with compassion, too.
Know that it's coming and that you will be able to handle it.

In these situations, speaking kindly to ourselves may seem
insincere, especially when we're disappointed in ourselves.
Yet we believe the negative self-talk as if it were gospel. We
question our self-kindness but rarely our self-judgment. *I
didn't have any answer to the question that came up in the meeting. I look so stupid.* Self-compassion allows us to reexamine
our bias toward critical voices and more objectively contrast
them against a gentler framing: *You're not good enough* versus *You're human.*

If you're feeling resistant to self-kindness and compassion
as you read this, work with this resistance. It's there to teach
you something about yourself. Psychologist Laura Silberstein-
Tirch invites people to ask themselves what functions self-criticism and judgment are serving: If you could wave a magic
wand and never beat yourself up again, what would be your
greatest fear?[56] This can often bring the stories we've been
telling ourselves to the surface. Maybe you feel that your drive
and work ethic come from holding yourself to high standards
and beating yourself up if you don't meet them. This is the
energy drink approach to leadership, which may hype you up
for a short time and result in some immediate successes but
leaves you drained and unable to function in the long term.

If you're reading this book, you're likely a successful leader
with years or decades of expertise, deep industry knowledge, and a powerful network. You've demonstrated your

capabilities through your drive, hard work, determination, and, possibly, perfectionistic streak. Maybe you're fueled by a chip on your shoulder or a desire to prove your worth.

One of my clients who heads a successful sales organization told me they often seek candidates who seem to have something to prove, candidates with a proverbial chip on their shoulder. As a Seattle native, my mind immediately recalled the 2014 Super Bowl.

The Seattle Seahawks coach Pete Carroll had a reputation for discovering the overlooked and the underestimated—diamonds in the rough. He sought players who'd been snubbed or discarded by other teams. He saw potential in these underdogs. Seahawks quarterback Russell Wilson, for instance, was a mere fifth-round pick, largely due to concerns about his height. And some of the squad? They weren't even drafted—a slight they proudly converted into high-performance fuel, eventually winning the Super Bowl.

A chip on the shoulder can be a potent motivator. It can inspire someone to defy expectations, challenge the status quo, and obliterate barriers. However, it's a double-edged sword. That same chip can come out as bitterness, a perpetual sense of victimhood, or an unyielding sense of martyrdom.

In essence, "a chip on the shoulder" suggests a sense of grievance, a feeling that you've been dealt an injustice that you can't shake off. It all boils down to motivation. What stokes your fire? Is it a desire to prove naysayers wrong, or a drive to validate your own beliefs and capabilities? While this chip can be a powerful asset, it's crucial to understand its origins. Ask yourself: Who are you trying to prove your worth to? And most important, why does it matter? Do you secretly still believe that if you no longer beat yourself up or pause to examine ambition veering into destructive compulsion, you'll lose your edge? If you're nodding right now, you may be on a path that leads to a dead end or total burnout.

In the initial stages of your career, technical and functional expertise were paramount. You delivered high-quality work and ascended through the ranks, but then the expectation subtly shifted: Can you enable others to deliver? Now your role is not just to lead, but to develop a new crop of leaders in their own right.

The belief in achievement, perfection, control, and an unwavering commitment to your field has undoubtedly served you well. However, you'll eventually encounter a pivotal moment where you must find the courage to let go of the familiar. Motivation through self-kindness is a much gentler and slower experience that doesn't fit with the old ideas of leadership and success built on breakneck speed and muscling through, eyes squinting and teeth gritted the whole time. Self-compassionate leadership is an invitation to release what has brought previous successes and accolades to usher in the next chapter of leadership and personal evolution.

THE ORGANIZATIONAL ATHLETE

When you're feeling resistant to self-compassion, asking for support, or relying on others, it can be helpful to think of yourself as an organizational athlete. We sometimes perceive athletes as lone wolves who push through pain and adversity to reach incredible heights apart from the rest of the pack. While it's true that star athletes usually possess a rare combination of massive talent and an incredible work ethic, we often forget that they never go it alone.

They rely not only on their teams, but on all kinds of different coaches and support staff, including massage therapists, dieticians, and trainers. A variety of experts help athletes reach their peak-level performance, offering assistance on everything from mastering particular skills and techniques to changing lifestyle habits such as nutrition and sleep, building mental resilience, and creating a high-performance mindset. Don't just take it from me. One of the best to ever play in the NBA, LeBron James reportedly spends seven figures a year on his body, mind, and spirit to maintain peak performance. While 99 percent of us don't have that kind of budget, the principle still applies.

When we start to think of ourselves as organizational athletes, we understand that we need to ask for help, guidance, and expertise from others to address our gaps in knowledge, skill, or perspective. And, most important, we need to take that theoretical knowledge, instruction, and guidance and practice it every day. Self-compassion helps us become more self-aware while also supporting us in dealing with the difficult truths and realities we discover.

We can make a positive change once we're truthful about what we need to address—sleep and rest, diet and nutrition, movement and exercise, meditation and mindfulness, false narratives and mindset, process and projects, relationships and communication, or strategy and performance.

We learn to strike a delicate balance between theoretical education, training, performance, and recovery. We learn that self-kindness is not a vague concept or a self-indulgent escape hatch but the most effective practice when it comes to building our best selves.

SEPARATE ACTION FROM EMOTION TO MANAGE RESISTANCE

It's important to remember that the act of self-compassion doesn't require good or happy feelings. As we've discussed, self-compassion may feel quite uncomfortable at first; it may even bring up difficult feelings. Especially when practicing self-kindness as a leader, it's good to remember that this practice isn't dependent on how you feel about it. You can feel your resistance and do it anyway!

Joseph Goldstein, a prominent figure in the field of contemporary mindfulness and meditation practices, introduced the concept of "mental rope burn" to describe the psychological and emotional discomfort that arises when we cling too tightly to our feelings and thoughts.[57] Just as holding on too tightly to a moving rope can cause a physical rope burn, mentally clinging to our feelings or thoughts can lead to emotional pain. Goldstein suggests that much of our suffering is self-created through our resistance to what's happening in the present moment. When we hold onto our feelings, whether they're positive or negative, we prevent ourselves from experiencing the natural flow of emotions. This clinging can show up as obsession over past events, worry about the future, or inability to let go of anger or sadness.

The keys to avoiding this mental rope burn are awareness and acceptance. By being aware, we can observe our thoughts and feelings without getting entangled in them. This means recognizing our emotions and thoughts as they arise but not attaching ourselves to them or allowing them to dictate our actions. Instead, we learn to let these feelings come and go, experiencing them fully but not holding onto them. This approach does not mean becoming indifferent or detached from our emotions. Instead, it's about developing a healthier relationship with our thoughts and feelings. It's about recognizing that while we cannot always control what we feel, we can control how we respond to these feelings. In this way, mindfulness practice helps reduce emotional and psychological distress—the mental rope burn—that comes from clinging too tightly to our inner experience.

This concept frees you up to be kind to yourself without first experiencing happy emotions to motivate you to treat yourself well. Waiting for inspiration in the form of feelings of kindness and love toward ourselves can keep us stuck in an endless loop. Knowing that we can act kindly toward ourselves without being prompted by positive feelings to do so can be liberating. This is different from faking it until you make it. You're not pretending that you are or feel different. You're simply separating your actions from your emotions. Self-kindness requires no good feelings, just goodwill, as Kristin Neff reminds us.[58]

YOUR TWO BEST FRIENDS

Self-compassion is like having a trusted friend who can shake you up as well as make you smile. And you value this friend. As Kristin Neff asserts, self-kindness is both tender and fierce.[59] I think of it as comfort and courage, leeward and windward. You can think of these polarities of self-kindness as your two best friends. The one who provides support and a soft shoulder

LEEWARD/COMFORT	WINDWARD/COURAGE
Self-care	Accountability
Regulation	Activation
Rest	Energy
Ship in the harbor	Ship in the storm
Tender	Fierce
Validation	Empowerment

FIGURE 13. Leeward/Comfort and Windward/Courage. The tension of leeward/comfort and windward/courage can look like this in practice.

to cry on, and the one who goes to bat for you, stands up to the bullies, and advocates for you. You need the therapist who validates you as much as the coach who empowers you. A good pal will lend a friendly ear when you're having a hard time, and they will call you on your bullshit when you've been complaining about the same damn thing for months.

You need both of these friends in your corner and both of these aspects of self-kindness to strike the right balance between acceptance and activation. Working with the Ward Model on finding the right mix of courage and comfort is akin to discerning when you need each of your two best friends and how to make the most of each distinct type of support they offer (figure 13).

Embracing ourselves with exactly the type of care and self-kindness we need in any given situation can be nothing short of transformative in allowing us to achieve true accountability in our lives. Continually practicing awareness, acceptance, and accountability will guide us in our evolution to becoming a self-compassionate leader.

7 » **PERFECTLY IMPERFECT**

How to Practice Progress

The greatest gap in the world is the gap between knowing and doing.

JOHN MAXWELL, *Fifteen Invaluable Laws of Growth*

Carlos was a self-described people pleaser when we met, always looking for others' approval and appreciation of his hard work. He wanted to be liked personally and respected professionally. At work, he was deeply frustrated by constantly having to pick up other people's slack and jump in to do their work, but he also derived great value from being the rescuer, fixer, and helper. He had little sense of self-worth and needed constant validation, with the result that he frequently did extra work without ever receiving the rewards he felt he was owed.

I asked Carlos to start an appreciation practice, naming three things he appreciated about himself every day. You may be familiar with gratitude practices that focus on what we're grateful for in our lives, but we rarely extend this appreciation to ourselves. This idea may feel too fluffy to you, but it works. The daily practice of affirming yourself for personality or character traits you authentically value helps reorient your focus from external affirmation to internal validation, resulting in higher self-worth. It's a slow process that brings incremental but lasting change.

I saw this progress with Carlos when he learned to say no because he didn't have the bandwidth, even if it made him uncomfortable not to accommodate the other person's request. As we kept working together, he saw improvements in more confrontational work situations. One day, he found himself spinning out of control during a strategy session with executives. He was anxious, feeling both unappreciated for his efforts and worried that he wasn't doing enough. The team was discussing a problem he felt the urge to fix instead of helping the group come to a consensus. He was itching to be the savior and frustrated nobody else saw what he considered an obvious solution. Instead of spiraling out of control, he excused himself and stepped out into the hallway to do a breathing exercise we'd practiced together.

EXERCISE » **The 4-7-8 Breathing Technique**

» Close your lips and inhale through your nose for a count of four.

» Hold your breath for a count of seven.

» Exhale completely through your mouth making a whoosh sound for a count of eight.

» Repeat three more times.

Afterward he didn't give himself a dramatic pep talk in the mirror, screaming, "You're awesome! You're the man!" As much as I loved Matthew McConaughey's *Wolf of Wall Street* performance, self-compassion isn't some kind of chest-pounding chant to pump yourself up. Rather, it's grounding yourself in the knowledge that you deserve to be in the room and at the table. Carlos reminded himself that he had value to add and worthwhile contributions to share.

Back in the meeting, he asked open-ended questions with genuine curiosity, which refocused the group on finding a solution together. He didn't have to go it alone, take over, fix anything, or rescue anyone. He acted like a true leader by regulating his nervous system so he could be fully present and curious and offer the guidance the team needed. While the outcome was ideal in this situation, the most meaningful progress for Carlos consisted of the way he handled himself. He acted like the leader he wanted to be, regardless of what happened once he stepped back into that room.

Deploying self-compassion makes us better individual leaders by making us more resilient, emotionally agile, regulated, and strong. However, we can make an even bigger difference once we decide to actively encourage and model self-compassion in our workplace and to our teams. How can you, as a leader, create an environment in your organization where others are inspired to practice compassion toward themselves and one another? This is where self-compassion truly moves beyond its benefits for you as an individual and a leader and starts to permeate your company's culture.

Every day we write our own story by how we move in the world and how we decide to respond to stimuli at the levels of our gut, heart, and mind. This is where our freedom and growth occur. It is our internal journey and struggle—facing our demons and processing our trauma, uncovering our values and purpose—that allow us to see ourselves and our lives with new eyes. It is primarily our inward state of being that impacts our outward expression. Especially in leadership capacities, progress comes from identifying our physical sensations, emotions and feelings, thoughts, ideas, and stories with self-compassion, so we can consciously determine how to act rather than getting stuck in endless reactive loops. We are better able to stand tall and hold strong convictions loosely, while creating an atmosphere of psychological safety in our organizations.

Deploying self-compassion in that gap between stimulus and response allows us to model to our employees, colleagues, teams, and companies how to balance humility, forgiveness, and confidence while avoiding imposter syndrome, impulsivity, people pleasing, and perfectionism.

REFUSING THE TYRANNY OF PERFECTION

When we refuse to submit to our perfectionist WIMP's chatter, we start to focus on what we *can*, rather than *can't*, achieve. Self-compassion allows us to view setbacks and discomfort as part of our shared human experience rather than an indictment of ourselves and our capabilities. As we let go of perfection, we are more open to accepting a nonlinear path to our goals. We have greater capacity to accept the frailty of life and the natural fallibility of people, including ourselves, while enhancing our resilience in the face of setbacks. Instead of being stuck in constant rumination about what we did or didn't do and what could go wrong, we focus more on what we're learning from these setbacks so we can continue to press forward.

Another way to look at it is to assume Adam Grant's scientist mind, as he explains in his book *Think Again*.[60] Acting as a scientist, according to Grant, means the willingness to question our assumptions and the openness to accept new information. This mindset helps us feel less defensive and more curious about the data points that arise in our lives, whether an accusation from a friend, a feeling of shame for failing at a project, or a self-limiting belief we can't shake. As Grant writes, When we're in scientist mode, "we refuse to let our ideas become ideologies."[61] We no longer connect our identity and who we are to a belief we hold or an idea we've come up with. Looking at a challenging incident through a scientist's lens helps us be both more objective and more forgiving, because we're less likely to see it as a personal failure and more as a situation to address. Grant explains: "You have to care more about improving yourself than proving yourself."[62]

TRUST YOURSELF TO TRUST YOUR TEAM

Researchers Yasuhiro Kotera and William Van Gordon reviewed the effects of self-compassion training on work-related well-being and found that "self-compassion activates an individual's soothing system (related to feeling safe, connected and cared for), as opposed to drive (related to excitement, striving and achieving) and threat (related to fear, anxiety and anger) systems that are more associated with mental distress."[63] In other words, self-compassion is a great predictor of well-being at work, because self-kindness helps us self-soothe the stress and difficulties that inevitably arise in work environments.

As a leader, it's up to you to model self-compassion and self-kindness to your team to ensure people will feel psychologically safe enough to be vulnerable themselves. Ask yourself how comfortable you are sharing your honest feelings with your team. If the idea alone makes you cringe, how will you be able to create space for someone else to express their feelings? Yes, this means bringing your whole self to work but without the inappropriate oversharing. Being fully human doesn't mean you need to be fully transparent in any situation. You'll still use judicious discernment on what types of disclosures are appropriate.

You may choose to let your team know that you're taking a few days off because your father died and that it's been difficult for you to focus on work while he's been in the hospital. But you'd likely keep it between you and your family, close friends, and therapist that you've had a contentious relationship with him for the last few years and are feeling guilty for not making amends or finding closure before his death. If you notice extremes—if, one the one hand, you're uncomfortable with vulnerability at any level or, on the other hand, you're acting as a therapist for your team members—you need to recalibrate.

Most important, remember that self-compassion isn't something you can fake; it will always come out in how you respond to others. If your team sees you beating yourself up about a failed project, they will be less likely to believe you're not upset about a costly mistake they made. And, of course, self-compassion should never be used to extract higher performance from your team. Encourage your employees to take their vacation days because they deserve the rest, not because you read a study that says vacation will make them more productive when they return. In other words, you can't pretend you've done the difficult inner work and are extending self-compassion to yourself and someone else without eventually slipping up. Don't turn faking self-compassion, or using it as the newest productivity tool, into your second full-time job!

EXERCISE » Reframing Outdated Leadership Clichés in Coaching

When dealing with bleak situations, leaders and coaches may default to dispensing catchphrase advice in the form of outdated leadership clichés steeped in toxic positivity. A conscious self-compassion practice requires questioning our tendency to accept these tropes and working to reframe them in helpful, realistic, and sustainable ways.

Even with a conscious self-compassion practice, we're creatures of habit, and it can take a while to stop using phrases that are embedded in our culture. Let's look at a few examples you may feel tempted to use with yourself or your team and options for reframing them:

» **Winning is the goal. Failure is not an option.** This catchphrase can create a fear of failure and stifle creativity and risk taking.

  » REFRAME: Failure is an opportunity for growth and success in the future.

» **You can do it, because I've done it before.** This phrase ignores the fact that everyone is an individual with different struggles and weaknesses.

  » REFRAME: Everyone's skills, abilities, and limitations are different and deserve customized support.

» **It could be worse. It's not that bad.** This phrase minimizes individual experiences by comparing them to potentially more challenging situations, which may invalidate genuine struggles.

  » REFRAME: This sucks. I'm sorry you're going through this difficult time.

» **Everything happens for a reason.** This phrase dismisses the validity of negative experiences and discourages meaningful reflection on adversity.

  » REFRAME: This setback isn't a punishment or just a lesson in finding the silver lining, but a complicated situation that I can learn from in my own time.

Try it for yourself by writing down three phrases you frequently use at work that could be considered toxic positivity, and reframe them using a self-compassionate leadership approach. Remember that self-compassionate leadership is about balance, about acknowledging the dark while orienting ourselves and our team toward the light. It's about accepting the fullness of human experience.

As Brené Brown explains in the HBO series *Atlas of the Heart*, based on her book of the same name, we can see emotion

in other people, but we can't fully understand their experience of it. We may project onto them how we'd feel in the
same situation or how we experience the emotion, but we'd
be wrong. Each person is coping with so much backstory, history, and life experience that we need to act with curiosity
rather than with assumptions or judgments based on our
own experience.

Often your job as a leader is to find solutions to problems.
You likely have come this far because you have good ideas
and sound decision-making skills, so it can be easy to get
aggravated if someone brings you a problem that you can
easily fix or that wouldn't exist in the first place if people
had handled it your way. At least, that's what you may think.
In cases like this, however, it's not enough to withhold toxic
positivity. One of the most effective ways self-compassion
can help you become a better leader is by making you more
curious than critical. Good leaders excel at problem solving. Great leaders guide others through problem solving for
themselves.

Genuine curiosity isn't about asking leading questions
that validate your proposed solution. Instead, true curiosity
means letting go of assumptions and seeking to understand
the other person, their emotions and thoughts, the challenges
they face, and the outcome they desire. We don't need to tell
them how to get to the outcome. We need to help them exca-
vate their true perspective on the situation so they can let go
of the feelings, thoughts, or behaviors that stand in their way
and find their own custom solution aligned with their desired
outcome.

GENUINE CURIOSITY IN LEADERSHIP

Here are the steps I take to ensure I help my clients fully unpack a situation:

1. **Reflect back what the other person is saying.** Reflecting
    means not paraphrasing or interpreting, but rather
    mirroring as best as you can, allowing your team
    member to reconsider whether that's exactly how they
    feel or think. If not, it opens the door to give them a
    second pass at digging deeper.

2. **Dig deeper by asking "And what else?"** This question
    from *The Coaching Habit* by Michael Bungay Stanier[64]
    is an open-ended invitation to dig deeper and explore
    related tangents.

3. **Accept emotions, don't accept stories.** I believe my
    clients when they tell me about their emotions and
    experience. I don't always believe the stories they tell
    about those emotions. Curiosity in coaching means
    inviting my clients to consider different perspectives,
    asking what else may be true in the situation,
    encouraging them to test their assumptions, and
    requiring them to challenge their thoughts.

Self-compassion fuels this genuine curiosity in several
ways: I don't need to stroke my own ego by solving problems
and being right, I care about validating my team member's
experiences, and I see my responsibility as coaching rather
than giving prescriptive advice.

Navigating Difficult Conversations without Burning Bridges

This compassionate and curious approach helps in another challenging aspect of leadership: difficult conversations. Whether you need to let someone go, put them on a performance plan, provide difficult feedback, or tell them they've been passed over for a promotion, it's natural to avoid those discussions—not because you're a bad person or leader but because you're trying to protect yourself, the other person, or both. You may find yourself reluctant because you want to be liked. Your people-pleaser WIMP may show up in full force, because, like all of us, you want to belong, fit in, and be regarded in a positive way. That's human nature. You don't need to beat yourself up about it, but you do need to pay attention when your need to be liked gets in the way of being a leader.

We have to extend self-kindness so we can do the hard thing instead of relying on our employees or reports to give us the affirmation we seek. We all want to be liked, but being a spineless nice guy is not a leadership philosophy—it's a cop-out. Sometimes difficult conversations will result in your employees feeling more supported and invested because they know you care enough to bring a concern to their attention. They might even respect and trust you more after that conversation because they know where they stand. And if they don't, it probably won't be worse than the anxiety you'd feel procrastinating the conversation.

When we get into a conflict of any kind, we typically fall

into fight, flight, freeze, or fawn mode—either aggressively attacking the other person, backing off, procrastinating, or hoping the situation will resolve itself. Often we don't take the alternative path of having difficult conversations and hearing the other person out, while deploying compassion toward both ourselves and the other person. This path leads toward a shared understanding of differing perspectives and desires for outcomes and an openness to achieving those outcomes. Self-compassion can help guide us through tough conversations without devolving into blame, sabotage, or escalation.

Cruelty Masquerading as "Brutal Honesty"

On the first day of a leadership workshop, the participants and I co-created the ground rules to ensure a productive and safe environment in which we could get a little messy, go deep, have fun, and learn together. One of the leaders in the room requested "brutal honesty" as a ground rule. I agreed with the honesty part but questioned why it needed to be brutal. As Brené Brown says, "clear is kind, and unclear is unkind."[65]

Sometimes honesty is painful to hear, but there is no reason to make it more brutal than it has to be. You may want to ask yourself whether you skew a little heavy on the brutal part and whether the honesty part could be delivered without it. If you secretly enjoy making it hurt just a little bit or think the other person deserves the sting, you're no longer serving the recipient or the situation. You're only serving yourself. That's got nothing to do with being an effective leader. That's just being an asshole.

The Other F Word—Feedback

Just the word "feedback" can be triggering for people. Most of us have experienced situations in which we received or offered feedback that hurt us or other people. These experiences can lead to resistance and avoidance when we face situations that require feedback. We may take feedback too personally and allow it to crush us, or we may reject it outright, even if there's truth in it that could increase our self-awareness. Leaders, in particular, may find themselves more comfortable in power differentials where they always dole out feedback but consider themselves above receiving it.

During the Hoffman Process, the leadership retreat I mentioned in the introduction, one of the group's guidelines was to refrain from talking about our professional lives or careers. I struggled hard with that instruction, but my discomfort quickly illustrated how much my identity was tied up with my professional persona. You may suspect this about yourself too, but it's a lot more normalized in American culture compared with other cultures. In the US, one of the first questions upon meeting someone new is typically "What do you do?" We are primed, encouraged, and conditioned to define ourselves through what we do for work.

This, I realized, was one of the primary reasons it was so hard for me to deal with feedback productively, whether I was giving or receiving it. I was conflating my *doing* with my *being*, and that made it difficult to separate myself from the feedback I received. I took it personally because I considered my work an intrinsic part of who I was. Since I conflated my professional role with my identity, I also conflated feedback about my role with feedback about my identity. If your boss worries about a project going badly, you might hear that you're a bad employee. If you receive feedback that you spoke too harshly to a coworker, you may consider yourself a mean person. How well feedback conversations go greatly depends on paying attention to our intent behind the message and the impact it has on the listener.

WOO-WOO WINS » Beck

Beck, a senior leader at a technology company, considered themself an achiever who acted as a servant leader. Unfortunately, anonymous 360 assessment feedback suggested that they rubbed peers the wrong way, especially because their communications with the senior team often had unintended negative impacts. Inward and outward, intent and impact, were not aligned. At first, Beck felt targeted by two specific people on their team, which caused resistance to looking deeper. The anonymous feedback revealed that one of Beck's blind spots was justifying their behavior and communication style.

Beck was a practitioner of mindful awareness, and over time their daily meditation provided the reflective space to become curious and look underneath their bravado: "The truth is I was arrogant in pursuit of my achievements. I'm a baller and didn't think anyone was of the same caliber. I considered myself in a different league." It was hard to admit the truth.

Self-compassion helped Beck see more clearly that their hard-charging, go-getter persona came with an underbelly of arrogance and condescension while helping them understand the origins of that behavior and forgive themself for it. "As an LGBTQ person, I grew up as a member of an underrepresented group. I also had a learning difference, dyslexia. I always felt the need to prove myself. I was othered in so many ways—a misfit different from everyone else. I had to work harder because of my dyslexia. I had to climb a steep hill as an LGBTQ individual, and I got value out of achieving against all odds. I didn't realize that my legitimate resentment at having to do so much more to earn the same level of success resulted in a huge chip on my shoulder."

Self-compassion and mindfulness helped Beck to love themself regardless of outward achievements, just for being who they were. This, in turn, allowed them to approach communicating with their peers in a more humble and grounded way. Because self-compassion taught them that they were loved, loving, and lovable, they no longer had to inflate their ego or prove they were better than everyone else. They could accept their own humanity and, therefore, everyone else's. Beck's communication approach now mirrored their intent, which led to much more positive interactions and relationships with people at work and at home.

COMMUNICATION 2.0: INTENT AND IMPACT

As George Bernard Shaw so eloquently reminds us, "The single biggest problem with communication is the illusion that it has taken place." Identifying and navigating intent and impact makes communication incredibly complex.

First, of course, we must ask whether we truly have positive intent. Only you can know the truth. I've certainly been in situations where I've proclaimed positive intent, but I've actually felt irritated, defensive, or even angry. If we notice that our true intent is to belittle or defend, to fight, manipulate, or coerce, we need to step back and realign our gut, heart, and mind to the task at hand. Whether you need to take a break to get some air, dig deeper into your feeling of defensiveness, or challenge your story about the other party's character, do it *before* attempting to communicate. This is a good time to do a breathing exercise, get a snack or some water, go for a quick walk, make notes on the feedback you want to communicate rather than winging it, or move the discussion to another day when you've had a chance to sleep on it.

POSITIVE INTENT ≠ POSITIVE IMPACT

Even if you have the best intentions, the impact of your communication can be an unwelcome surprise. Your positive intent does not automatically mean your communication will have a positive impact. This is obvious, but we forget it all the time. I have to remind myself that everyone comes with a unique background, life experience, and current physical, emotional, and mental state. Even with positive intent, I can't guarantee how my communication will land with the other person.

As leaders, we must take responsibility for closing the gap between intent and impact as much as possible. The first step here is to avoid holding onto our intent too desperately. As a manager or leader, I have done that many times, defending my positive intent even if the impact was less than desirable. Being too focused on explaining that I came from a good place made me blind to the words I chose, the tone, or the setting that might have skewed the impact.

When I was facilitating leadership development workshops for a previous employer, I mentored a direct report who was my potential successor. We were traveling around the country, running leadership programs together, and I thought they did a great job. I wanted to support them in their path to becoming a lead facilitator, and my intention was to continually give them more responsibility to prepare for that role. The colleague had communicated an interest in the opportunity, so I tried to help them hone their presentation skills, communication, and executive presence.

However, the impact was quite the opposite. My colleague felt that I was trying to make them more like me instead of encouraging them to get better at the tasks while honing their own voice. No matter how good my intentions, my words and actions ended up eroding trust instead of building it. My colleague received the message that what they were doing wasn't good enough and that "good enough" had to be my way, not theirs. It wasn't the message I tried to send, but that's how it landed. If I were in that situation today, I would worry less about my intent and more about my impact. I would be more curious and ask my colleague why my efforts were landing that way and what I could do to improve our collaboration and communication in the future.

As leaders who are trying to build the next generation of leaders, we need to recognize that our impact is crucial.

Positive intent is important, but if it doesn't effectively create the desired impact, it's meaningless.

NEGATIVE IMPACT MAY NOT BE YOUR FAULT, BUT IT IS YOUR RESPONSIBILITY

Self-compassion can help us see that even if we're doing our best and our heart is in the right place, our impact can be negative, and it doesn't have to be anyone's fault. Self-compassion allows us to gently question whether our intent is truly positive. Self-compassion can also be invaluable in forgiving ourselves when even our best effort causes damage from time to time. In that situation, self-compassion can help us refrain from judging ourselves or the other person and instead focus on how to rectify the situation. What can we do to solve the communication issue? How can we relate to each other to build trust? How can we support each other successfully?

Self-compassion can even help us have uncomfortable conversations in the moment. If you're clear on your intent, you can likely tell by the other person's facial expression, change in tone, or body language when your message is not landing as you'd hoped. Instead of continuing, you can take a moment to level with the other person, clarify your intent, and ask if it's coming across as you meant. If not, why? Of course, there are situations, especially when a power differential is involved, when it's difficult to speak up in real time. That's a primary reason why it's essential for leaders to be extremely aware and come back to conversations that seemed off. If you're the one with the power, then you have the greater responsibility to address potential issues and reconcile your intent and impact. Here are some examples of questions you can ask yourself and/or the other person:

» "Is my intent genuine, or is there another agenda hiding under what I've proclaimed as good intent?"

» "I assume you had positive intent when you said X. However, the impact of those words was hurtful. Can you please clarify?"

» "It seems we're not understanding each other in this situation. What is your intent for this conversation, and what is your preferred outcome?"

» "I noticed your tone / facial expression / body language change when I said X. Would you be willing to share your feelings / thoughts resulting from what I said at that moment?"

In sum, deploying compassion toward ourselves and others helps keep everyone's intent and impact in perspective, so we don't get hung up on whose fault a situation is and instead focus on how to find a solution and try again.

HOW SELF-COMPASSION HELPS YOU REACH YOUR GOALS

This focus on progress, not perfection, and on letting self-compassion guide our coaching and communication with our team members points the way to how we set individual, team, and companywide goals. The following series of questions helps us look beyond our immediate goals to figure out the big-picture outcomes we desire and why. As you ask yourself

"Why?" after each of these initial questions, this second inquiry will allow you to go deeper in connecting to your own
motivations.

» What is behind my goal? Why?

» What benefit is tied to the outcome I desire? Why?

» How do I want to show up differently as a leader? Why?

» How do I want my team to show up differently as leaders?
Why?

» How do we want our leadership to impact our organization, community, clients, and industry? Why?

In a *Harvard Business Review* article entitled "To Reach Your
Goals, Embrace Self-Compassion," Elizabeth Saunders explains that self-compassion helps us reach our goals because it
normalizes the negative feelings associated with the process.[66]
I recently asked my ten-year-old son Luca why he resisted
taking extra lessons to help develop his soccer skills. He told
me that running drills and getting coached is uncomfortable
because he's not that good at it. I empathized with his struggle
and reassured him that I often felt the same. I explained that
getting comfortable with being uncomfortable was one of the
best life skills to master because it allows us to learn anything.

Adopting a growth mindset and focusing on gradual progress helps us reach our goals. Rarely is our progress toward
a goal linear, and we almost always need to reckon with detours and setbacks that reek of failure. Self-compassion helps
us create goals in the face of failure and risk. It teaches us
how to cope with inevitable difficulties and stay the course
instead of giving up.

Like your values, your goals should connect with you on a deep, personal level. It's hard to stick with working toward any goal, so your goal must be one that is profoundly personal and aligned with your deepest values. Forget business jargon and buzzwords, and instead use your own language, phrasing, and words to represent a goal that sounds like you and elicits an emotional response. My friend and author Scott Shute calls this a "full body yes."[67] If it doesn't inspire you because it's not tied to your values or doesn't motivate you because it's not connected to your purpose, it won't matter enough to trigger action and commitment.

If you find yourself too wrapped up in work, a generic goal may be to stop working every day at 5:30 p.m. By making it personal, you can reframe the goal more specifically: *I will stop working at 5:30 p.m. every day, so I can be home on time to help my daughters with their homework, exercise, or spend time with my best friend.* Connect the goal to your deeper values and purpose. Setting good boundaries around how long you work and ensuring you get enough rest is a great goal. However, making your goal personal will remind you of *why* you want to set work boundaries in the first place, whether it's to cultivate relationships, take care of yourself, or learn something new. The specifics are what speak to your true values and purpose.

INCREASE THE POTENTIAL FOR SUCCESS

In her article, Saunders suggests using if/then statements to plan for detours and bumps in the road. *If X happens, then I will do Y.* This strategy has been shown to lead to greater success for all types of different goals. For example, if I feel alone, then I will reach out to a trusted friend and ask them about their experience. If I'm being ruthlessly harsh on myself, then I will stop and practice an act of self-kindness. If I'm emotionally triggered in a meeting, then I'll take a beat and ask myself, what's this emotion telling me?

Regardless of how small or big the goal is, we will encounter barriers along the way. Having an idea of how we'll deal with the most common pitfalls or situations we've encountered previously can take a little bit of the sting or shock out of the situation and help us focus on the mitigating next step to take. It is easy to retreat from action back into theory when things aren't going well. There is safety in analysis and planning. There is risk in taking the first step and not knowing whether you can get back up once you inevitably stumble. Going in with the expectation that we'll need to give ourselves space for grace, missteps, challenges, and errors encourages us to be more prepared for the things we *can* control and more accepting of the things we *can't* control. In other words, we're more likely to remain in an action- or practice-focused mindset that allows us to take time to recalibrate or adjust, without the threat of giving up or stopping altogether.

WOO-WOO WINS » Sarah

"If I don't promote them, will they leave? If I do promote them, will they fail?" My client Sarah went back and forth on the right move with regard to a person she was considering for promotion.

As a senior vice president in her organization's finance department, she was overworked and under-resourced and desperately needed someone to step up and take on more day-to-day responsibility so she could focus on strategy. Sarah had concerns about whether this person was ready to move into a director role, and she was clear about the technical skills and capabilities the prospect needed to improve upon. However, when it came to "soft" skills, the issues seemed more ambiguous. "I want them to speak up more in meetings," Sarah said. I recalled a class in which my teacher had wanted each student to contribute at least twice a day, so most of us just raised our hands twice to check the box. We didn't necessarily provide the outcome the teacher was likely trying to inspire: consistently engaging with the content, asking questions, making connections, and contributing our viewpoints.

I had a hunch that my client wasn't looking for her prospect to meet some arbitrary comment quota in meetings. So I asked about her reasoning behind this request and her desired outcome for the situation. I invited her to forget about hard skills and soft skills and instead to just think in terms of human skills. These skills are critical in every relationship, every team, every project, and every organization because they're about community and connection, belonging and collaboration, communication and transparency.

Considering the issue through this lens helped Sarah dig deeper into the big picture moves she needed this prospect to make. She realized that the outcome she needed wasn't really someone who was more vocal in meetings. That was merely a flimsy representation of the goal she truly wanted to achieve: developing a director who was willing to take charge by positioning themself as a leader within the team and proactively building trust and connections so that employees

would consider them the natural go-to for problems and challenges. Once we figured out what my client needed from her
prospect, we could pivot to discussing how she could deploy
self-compassion to come up with the steps necessary to make
that outcome a reality and support her new director in their
role.

It's helpful to think of goal achievement in three buckets: context, process, and outcome. Slicing it different ways allows
us to inhabit various perspectives on the situation to get a
comprehensive understanding of what's preventing us from
reaching our desired outcomes.

Context: The Situations and Relationships in Play

Self-compassion gave my client Sarah the opportunity to see
where her expectations hadn't been clear and where she
needed to provide more specific direction to the prospect. She
realized that some of the frustration of the situation was of
her own making. She was mostly annoyed with herself for
not being able to make this decision quickly and not understanding the questions she needed to ask herself to make a
sound decision. Once she used self-compassion to challenge
her feelings and get clear on her desired outcomes, she was
able to see the situation more realistically and adopt behaviors that strengthened rather than weakened her relationship
with her prospect.

Process: The Actions We Will Take

Sarah was able to practice compassion toward her prospect
after treating herself with compassion first. Her newfound

clarity on her desired goals and outcomes made it easier to transparently communicate her needs and wants to the prospect. She was able to provide clear direction and guidelines for accountability so that the prospect understood how and when to deliver on those expectations.

Outcome: The Specific Goal We Want to Achieve

The desired outcome for Sarah was establishing a director role to deal with day-to-day responsibilities so that she could free up her time for more strategic initiatives. Her outcome in choosing to promote this particular prospect was to set clear expectations, and then support them in their new role and set them up for long-term success. The context and process were in alignment with these goals and outcomes, after my client used self-compassion to challenge her own feelings about the situation and better understand her prospect's perspective.

CELEBRATE PROGRESS

Setting goals, of course, orients us toward the completion of said goal, so it's extremely important to mark milestones and celebrate progress. Fixating only on the end result can blind us to beautiful lessons on the path itself.

If you're solely focused on getting a promotion, it will be intensely frustrating if you don't get it. If, instead, you focus on the process it takes to get that promotion, such as delivering improved results, looking for opportunities to push yourself toward growth, thinking about the next small step to take toward your goal, and understanding what you do and don't have control over, you'll get much more out of the experience. Taking action on what you can control and letting go

of the rest—the outcome, such as the promotion—increases
the likelihood that you will achieve the promotion you want
but also ensures that you will make immense personal and
professional progress regardless.

Progress means measuring the gain, not the gap, as author
Dan Sullivan advises. By focusing on how we've grown, we
will encourage more forward momentum instead of ponder-
ing our failures.[68] This self-compassionate approach centers
on growth, not perfection, and creates internal strength and
resilience rather than depending on outside validation.

When you look to shorter-term targets and fractional goals,
you can celebrate as you go along. What have you accomplished so far? How has that impacted your team? What have
you learned? How much progress have you made? These
questions allow you to feel a sense of accomplishment and
greater agency over your process, which is especially crucial
when you're working on a seemingly insurmountable goal.

While writing this book, I have celebrated my progress on
writing each chapter as well as the phases of creation, publishing, and distribution, while having as much fun as I can
and integrating as many of the lessons as possible along the
way. The exercises and suggestions in this chapter are not
guarantees, but they are ways to prime yourself to center
self-compassion, stay emotionally regulated, and do everything in your power to create a productive environment for
growth and progress on a daily basis.

In the next chapter, we'll zoom out from the daily practice
of self-compassionate leadership to imagine what it could
look like to raise a new generation of leaders to transform
organizational culture as a whole.

8 » RIPPLE EFFECT

Tiny Transformations Lead to Massive Change

If you can't love yourself, how the hell you gonna love anybody else.

RUPAUL, drag queen and TV producer

Navy SEALs test themselves by "drown-proofing." Their feet are bound together, their hands are tied behind their backs, and they're thrown into a nine-foot-deep pool. Surprisingly, the key to their survival is not strength, endurance, or even their ability to swim. Author Mark Manson describes it like this: "The trick to drown-proofing is to actually let yourself sink to the bottom of the pool. From there, you lightly push yourself off the pool floor and let your momentum carry you back to the surface. Once there, you can grab a quick breath of air and start the whole process over again."[69] Our human instinct is to fight, to try to untie ourselves, to struggle for control. But to cope with the most difficult situations while keeping a sense of calm often means to stay with our fears until a solution shows itself. As Manson explains, "Instead of resisting the physics that would normally kill you, you must surrender to them and use them to save your own life."

Self-compassionate leadership is like drown-proofing yourself. What I've asked you to do in this book might feel counterintuitive in many ways, just like giving up the struggle and letting yourself sink. In those moments at the bottom of the pool (when your start-up fails, you get fired, or you lose everything you have), that's when self-compassion will be most valuable. It will give you that tiny space of peaceful resolve that allows you to calmly push off the bottom to get your head above water for a life-giving breath.

Outdated leadership philosophies, or how things have "always been done," are keeping us from reaching our full leadership potential and sometimes even threatening our health and lives. We have engineered emotional armor, external motivators, social comparisons, and beliefs that we are not enough. We need to start over and remember that we already are who we are trying to become—perfectly imperfect people sharing the human experience. Self-compassionate leadership is about going deeper to rework and rewire our outdated engineering. As the prolific leadership expert Marshall Goldsmith said, "What got you here won't get you there."[70] This statement is true with regard to not only our practice of leadership but also our beliefs and assumptions about our self-worth and belonging.

LETTING GO OF OLD WAYS TO REACH YOUR POTENTIAL

Maybe you've experienced consistent growth throughout your career, willing your way into positions of greater and greater responsibility and influence, all while carrying 50 pounds of "armor." The armor we put on piece by piece in adolescence and young adulthood is meant to keep us safe. The specific pieces of our armor may vary slightly, but they often include bravado and arrogance, defensiveness and aggression, coldness and detachment, or conflict avoidance and people pleasing. We try to project strength and confidence while trying to mask insecurity, vulnerability, and fear. We need this armor, we believe, to achieve success and fulfill our leadership potential.

In reality, emotional armor is not a benefit but a self-imposed limitation. It is precisely in accepting and embracing our shared humanity that we can connect to ourselves and everyone around us, in the process becoming truly great leaders. Some aspects of leadership that we think will help us fulfill our potential are actively damaging. We consider these things features when they're actually bugs. Although extreme competition, focus on external motivators, social comparison, and emotional repression do not help us reach our full potential as leaders in the long term, they're highly effective in bringing out our well-intentioned, misinformed protectors (WIMPs), causing imposter syndrome, an inability to give or receive critical feedback, a lack or overabundance of trust, or a failure to make necessary changes or decisions.

WOO-WOO WINS » Cassandra

I started coaching Cassandra, a senior engineering executive, after she was referred by her company's HR department for succession planning. During our work, she quickly realized that her hard-ass command-and-control leadership style was limiting her team's growth as well as her own. Still, she didn't want to lose her edge, believing the stoic, tough persona of her hard-ass WIMP was necessary for success. And yet, she constantly battled the urge to prove herself worthy of her position and feared that it would always be her alone against the world. She frequently expected the worst and secretly relished it when projects went wrong so she could step in and save the day. Being the hero and putting out fires made her feel worthy momentarily but left her drained and isolated.

After months of working on dismantling her armor piece by piece, Cassandra shared with me: "I realized my sharp edge was a persona to make me feel more confident. I now have let go of the need to have all the answers and to be perfect. I feel more confidence and less pressure than before. I'm having more fun in my work and life than I have in years, and the team is responding well. Recent feedback and performance are strong data points that this is working."

Self-compassion can help you remove the armor, and the emotional repression that comes with it, and replace it with a skill set that will allow you to stand in the headwinds of leadership. Self-compassion is not a cop-out when life gets hard. It's a way to navigate the human struggle gracefully and acknowledge who we are so we can be our best. But does this actually work in business, with your team, or while you're climbing the corporate ladder?

GET OFF THE HEDONIC
TREADMILL–FINALLY!

The concept of the "hedonic treadmill" suggests that individuals have a set point of happiness. When good or bad events happen, they may experience temporary increases or decreases in happiness, but over time they tend to return to their set point.[71] For example, after receiving a promotion or buying a new car, you might feel a boost in happiness, but this boost is often temporary, and you eventually return to your baseline level of well-being. This phenomenon inhibits long-term well-being because of three factors:

1. **Adaptation:** We quickly adapt to positive changes in our lives, making the derived pleasure short-lived.

2. **Relativity:** We compare our gains to those of others or to our own past, diminishing the impact of positive events.

3. **Endless pursuit:** The hedonic treadmill can lead us to relentlessly pursue fleeting pleasures while neglecting deeper, more sustainable sources of happiness.

Getting off the hedonic treadmill can help you reach your leadership potential. It sounds counterintuitive, but hear me out. Instead of constantly chasing the next big achievement or reward (which can lead to burnout and dissatisfaction), you will find greater satisfaction and well-being in fostering personal growth, building meaningful relationships, and pursuing a deeper sense of purpose in your work.

The Swedes have a concept known as *lagom*—"just the right amount." It means knowing when enough is enough. It allows you to practice finding balance, being content, and recognizing you have everything you need instead of constantly chasing more. *Lagom* helps you be the best leader you can be by discerning what is needed at any given moment. Truly sustainable leadership doesn't mean over- or underperforming but bringing "just the right amount."

SELF-COMPASSIONATE LEADERSHIP AS A CHANGE AGENT

When we learn to apply this approach to ourselves, we create the capacity to extend it to others and help them become more successful in turn. For their book *The Mind of the Leader*, authors Rasmus Hougaard and Jacqueline Carter surveyed more than 1,000 leaders. Although 92 percent of the leaders agreed that self-compassion is important or extremely important for effective leadership, the vast majority of them had no idea how to enhance their own self-compassion (80 percent).[72]

This book you hold in your hands has laid out the practices, exercises, and tools to change the game for you as a leader and for the next generation of leaders you will help develop and guide. A self-compassionate leader can be an agent of change for their team in crucial, practical ways, such as performance management and career development. When we give ourselves grace, accountability, support, and resources for our own growth, we model a healthy approach to improvement and evolution.

Self-compassionate leadership doesn't mean letting underperforming employees off the hook or remaining passive in the face of problems. Instead, self-compassionate leaders acknowledge the humanity of each team member and recognize that everyone has personal and professional struggles and deserves to work in an environment where resources and support are freely available. A leader's job is to understand and support their employees and invest in their growth—not just on paper and in fancy mission statements but in the real world. This may include difficult changes such as moving an employee into a different role, recommending training, or adjusting someone's scope of work or responsibilities to suit their current skills.

In her book *Promotions Are So Yesterday*, author Julie Winkle Giulioni introduces seven dimensions of employee development.[73] These seven dimensions include "climb," which refers to rising through the ranks, but it's complemented by six additional approaches to employee development: contribution, competence, confidence, connection, challenge, contentment, and choice.

This comprehensive framework goes beyond income, promotions, and titles and offers diverse avenues of personal and career development. Giulioni shares strategies to provide opportunities for employees to contribute within the organization, honoring the human need to make a difference, and ways to increase competence by enhancing critical skills, capabilities, and expertise. Connection gives team members a chance to become visible in the organization, create networks, and build relationships. Confidence is about leveraging employees' competence and connections to boost their trust in their talents so they can accept challenges to step up or get out of their comfort zone. This breeds contentment and enhances employees' ability to choose how to apply themselves at work and to select situations, teams, and projects that play to their strengths while also giving them opportunities for growth. Choices about when and how we work best are ever more crucial in our increasingly remote world. This self-compassionate approach to growth in the workplace helps individuals and organizations flourish and provides satisfaction, joy, and meaning. Moving away from a singular focus on money and titles encourages an organization-wide practice of compassion for self and others, collaboration instead of competition, constant evolution, and reciprocal generosity and support.

IT DOESN'T HAVE TO BE LONELY AT THE TOP

Leadership can be lonely for many reasons. The competitiveness that still pervades how we tend to see leadership might make you feel suspicious, even paranoid. You may suspect hidden agendas in every interaction or constantly scan your company for up-and-coming leaders who may be poised to take your spot. The inherent culture of scarcity often tied with leadership stipulates that once you've reached the top, there is no time to rest. Now you must expend as much or more energy maintaining, justifying, or defending your position.

In addition, leadership comes with external accolades, material benefits, social capital, power, and prestige that can make talking honestly about the many challenges come across as tone-deaf and entitled. The only other people who are likely to understand—other leaders—are your natural competitors, and it's hard to open up to people you see as the enemy. For top executives there may be no peers at all to confide in. As a coach I'm often the outlet for the executive who has few opportunities to open up to anyone with a compassionate, objective, and unencumbered ear. Self-compassion can combat the loneliness of leadership. It's an effective way for leaders to feel connected to the shared humanity among all people and the sense that many other leaders struggle with the same problems. Research shows the practice of self-compassion improves feelings of well-being, job satisfaction, and organizational prosocial behaviors, while decreasing emotional exhaustion and burnout.[74]

Self-compassion can help us belong, and this sense in turn rubs off on the people on our team. When people feel they belong in their workplace and do what they love, the results are higher engagement, resilience, and performance and lower turnover, according to a 2019 study from the ADP Research Institute.[75] Workers who reported they felt part of a team were not only 2.7 times more likely than others to be fully engaged, but also three times as likely to be resilient during challenges and twice as likely to report a strong sense of belonging in organizations. This collaborative approach to teams and organizations shows much more promise for true problem solving, leadership, and innovation than the leadership philosophies we were raised with.

EXERCISE » **Team Check-In**

Team-building exercises have long been embedded in corporate culture with varying success. One simple and effective way to translate self-compassion into leadership practice in a team setting is this simple exercise:

1. Each person in the meeting shares a recent win, or an accomplishment they feel good about or proud of. This increases the team member's trust in their own capabilities and, as they listen to others, in the capabilities of the team and organization. We often focus on supporting each other through hard times, but it's just as important to celebrate one another's successes.

2. Each person in the meeting shares a recent failure or mistake. It may be significant or fairly small—for example, maybe a project that didn't go as well as planned. Regardless of the specific problem shared, the focus should be on the lesson the person learned that helped them grow as a leader. What did they learn about themselves and their leadership approach? What will they do differently as a result? This helps remind everyone of their shared humanity and normalizes struggles and challenges.

3. Each person receives support from the team. In this last step, the entire team brainstorms how to support the team member through their challenge. Start by having each person think of a current and unresolved challenge they're facing, something they're stuck on. If, for example, I receive feedback that my presentations sound too rehearsed and that I'm too long-winded, I may address this by using bullet points instead of scripts, practice speaking more extemporaneously, and add more of my personality to presentations. The team might offer to support me by providing situational feedback when I'm showing progress or letting me know if they

see areas where there's still room for improvement. The point of this is not for the team to point out more failures, but for everyone involved to get a sense that they're all in it together, helping each other grow and evolve, and investing in each other as both people and professionals.

Level-Up Variation

The above exercise is a great way to start out with a new team but can soon start to feel superficial. We all have likely been in a team meeting where people claim their big failure that week was a presentation that could have gone better. Who cares? If you're ready to dig deeper with your team, try this option developed by Troika Consulting:[76]

» Split a bigger team into groups of three or four people.

» The first person has two minutes to explain their problem.

» The two or three team members then have two minutes to ask clarifying questions about the problem.

» The first person turns their chair around (or turns off their camera on Zoom), and the remaining teammates discuss the problem for four minutes as if the first person weren't present. The first person doesn't interject ("I already tried that!" "That would never work!") but only listens.

» The first person faces the group again (or turns on their camera) and takes one minute to share what they'll take away from the team discussion to address their problem.

» Repeat with every team member.

The beauty of this exercise variation is that it liberates a small team to truly think outside the box and brainstorm new solutions. The brainstorming team members are not restrained by the first person's interjections or dismissal. This freedom often leads to breakthroughs. I've engaged many leadership teams in this exercise, and they almost always report that it's incredibly helpful and brings up insights the person hadn't considered before. This method builds trust, appreciation, and respect among teams because it helps us leverage other people's expertise and ideas. We realize that sometimes we need not an expert but invested team members who think differently and can show us a new perspective.

PUNISHMENT VERSUS POSITIVE REINFORCEMENT

The old loss and punishment model was never going to work in the long term. As leadership coaches Marcos Cajina Heinzkill and Gregory Stebbins explain, "Many people believe that distress, discomfort, and pressure ignite performance."[77] However, these ideas and resulting behaviors are "toxic in nature, ineffective, unsustainable, and lead to burnout and career derailment." As I've laid out in this book, outdated leadership models are great at producing external results, but they leave us self-critical, judgmental, defensive, stuck, and underappreciated. Let's take a moment to think of the internal transformation you have made while reading this book. It doesn't have to be lofty or grand. Just questioning one limiting belief you've been taught, becoming aware of one of your WIMPs, or realizing when you've been working your second job of "covering" instead of your actual job—each of these is a tiny but profound transformation.

Are you finally tired of feeling the need to control everything and everyone around you? Are you ready to give up your relentless drive to be right all the time and expect perfection in an imperfect world of flawed humans, including yourself? Have you tried any of the activities or exercises and felt a moment of relief? Has a question on one of the lists sparked a memory or a dream for yourself? If the answer is yes, then self-compassion is already working to shift your focus from punishment and loss mindsets to a positive, growth-oriented approach.

We tend to think that positive reinforcement is an acceptable strategy in parenting but not in leadership development. It sounds too much like sticker charts and earning trips to the zoo. When it comes to high performance at work, too often we think the coach who yells at his players in the locker room is more likely to win than, for instance, TV character and soccer coach Ted Lasso, who cheers on his team with kindness and bakes biscuits for the boss. Research shows it takes only a week for lab rats to learn protective behaviors against punishment but three weeks to learn how to get the reward.[78] In other words, it takes lab rats three times longer to learn through positive reinforcement. We're not rats, but our brains work similarly: we try to avoid losses and punishments at all costs and are much slower to learn through positive reinforcement.

The first approach is fear-based, often resulting in short-term high-level performance because our brains have evolved to avoid pain and punishment. The second approach relies on purpose, value alignment, and a practice of self-compassion. It takes longer to learn because it's not our default mode. It will feel uncomfortable, but it leads to long-term success, partly because self-compassion motivates us to improve ourselves and facilitates our "goal pursuit by promoting a growth-oriented attitude and belief in our ability to change."[79]

ASSET-BASED LEADERSHIP

Once you start modeling self-compassionate leadership and it begins to spread among your team members, you'll see your organizational culture change. One of the most practical ways self-compassion can affect how you lead others and how they respond is in the context of change management.

Change management can look different in every company, but it usually includes managing changes in processes, technologies, and people to help the company reach its overall goals. It aims to support the implementation of changes during transition periods. Change management, however, can be a triggering term, not because change is necessarily bad but because so many organizations do it poorly, focusing on processes and technologies while forgetting about the people affected by change.

A self-compassionate leadership practice can put the focus back on a company's most precious asset: its people. This approach helps leaders empathize with employees struggling through transition phases and adapting to change. The more an organization builds capacity for self-compassion in its leadership and employees, the more everyone's ability to deal with challenges, change, and bumps in the road will grow.

Everyone will improve in their ability to manage emotions, self-soothe and regulate, and handle changes with grace and patience. When compassion is put at the center of the change initiative, it empowers team members to become change agents for themselves and each other. Asset-based leadership focuses on the strengths and resources of an organization or team rather than solely on its weaknesses and challenges. It's about recognizing and using the positive aspects of an organization to create value and achieve goals. As author and documentarian Douglas Rushkoff writes, "Instead of focusing on what we still lack, we must take stock of what we already do have in terms of resources, abilities, and pure will." Asset-based thinking is anchored in reality and focuses on what we can do with what we have. *What are our assets? What is working? How might we apply this resource in a new way? How can we leverage X to reach goal Y?*

This asset-based approach better equips you to guide your teams and organizations to success by helping you

» **Build a positive culture:** By focusing on the strengths of your organization, you can create a positive and optimistic environment that motivates and inspires your team.

» **Foster innovation:** By identifying and leveraging the assets of your organization, you can find new and creative ways to tackle challenges and generate ideas.

» **Develop resilience:** When you focus on your assets, you are better equipped to withstand challenges and setbacks. This resilience can help organizations navigate tough times and emerge stronger.

» **Attract and retain talent:** An asset-based approach to leadership can create a sense of pride and purpose in employees, which can help attract and retain top talent.

In line with self-compassionate leadership, asset-based thinking neither denies reality nor focuses on what a person or organization is lacking or can't control. Instead, it centers on a realistic appraisal of individual and organizational strengths to achieve goals and create a resilient and innovative culture.

WOO-WOO WINS » Sailplane

Many companies and their leaders operate with the product, customers, investors, and technology at the core of all decision-making. Especially now, with AI taking over many aspects of business, we need to be part of the movement toward self-compassionate leadership that elevates human intelligence (HI). Sailplane is doing just that.

Sam Ramji, whom you first met in chapter 2 taking some time off after a brutal 360 assessment, eventually became Sailplane's co-founder and CEO. His central philosophy in founding Sailplane was to advance the future of human work by using AI to support HI. The move from computation to cognition presents opportunities to flip the script between AI and HI. At Sailplane, people are placed back in the center, with technology there to support humanity, not the other way around. Sailplane is building a human-centric culture from the ground up, aligning people around a central set of principles and ethics. Sam is leaning into kindness as a strength, not a weakness: "I'm nice, and I enjoy being nice. Thomas the Tank Engine is my spirit animal. My goal is to be kind, helpful, and useful, to be in service of others and my communities, not solely myself."

Sailplane defines human intelligence as different from artificial intelligence in three key ways:

1. **Curiosity:** Humans ask questions about the meaning and subtext of reality and consciousness.

2. **Creativity:** Humans generate truly new ideas.

3. **Care:** Humans show empathy and compassion to others in recognition of our shared humanity.

Sam's goal with Sailplane is to build a place he wants to be—a company inspired by his interactions with the environment, the people he works with, and what he considers meaningful work. Getting to choose our identities at work ultimately changes the truth of who we are in the world.

HUMANS ARE NOT MACHINES

Elevated leadership flows from the fact that we're learning how to fully embrace our complex humanity. This isn't done solely by reading books, taking classes, and discussing the merits of self-compassion. It must become a daily practice, the aggregate of a thousand tiny changes and small kindnesses that we dedicate ourselves to again and again.

Practicing self-compassion in our personal lives inevitably transforms us as leaders because it first changes us as humans. As I was writing this book, I was fortunate to interview leadership coach Bob Dunham, who founded the Institute for Generative Leadership, a beacon of transformative thinking in today's mechanistic world. He's been working tirelessly to center humanity in leadership discourse and practice.

The current prevailing metaphor for action is the machine. Unwittingly, many of us have become entangled in this narrative: one that demands we function like well-oiled gears, chasing perfection and performance. Not only do we view ourselves as machines, but we also perceive others through the same cold, mechanistic lens.

Leadership, in too many organizations, boils down to ensuring that these "machines" operate at peak performance. This perspective grossly undermines our true nature. It fails to recognize our complexities, our histories, our spiritual depths, and the vast sea of emotions that make us human. It also misses the point that human beings who are treated with dignity in an environment that cultivates their human virtues vastly outperform machines both individually and together in networks of coordination.

The mechanistic view lauds our sacrifice of time and well-being as a noble act. But what are we really sacrificing? Our very humanity. Our ability to show compassion, to understand our inner selves, and to appreciate the intricacies of human life. By placing unwavering emphasis on external results, we've inadvertently sidelined our physical, mental, emotional, and spiritual well-being. Our external results are shaped by the quality of our internal states, and connecting the two is where leadership meets community.

The underpinnings of generative leadership are deeply rooted in speech act theory, pioneered by Oxford professor

John Austin in the 1940s.[80] Austin's groundbreaking work highlighted that language goes beyond mere description; it has the power to create. When you make a request or a promise, you're not merely labeling an action, you're enacting one. You're shaping the future. This act of creation through speech is the essence of generative leadership—molding the future not just by speaking of it but by speaking it into existence.

During our interview, Dunham offered me a declaration exercise that deeply resonated with me, given my own struggle with accepting my humanity and my tendency to pursue mechanistic perfectionism. I invite you to follow Bob's instructions and read the declaration out loud. I offer it as a parting gift from Bob and me at the close of this book.

Take a deep breath, and settle back in your chair. Open your chest, and let yourself have this moment. Put any assessment of what we're doing out of your mind, and just go with the experience of it. Let the words I give you come from inside of you and hold meaning. Read these words aloud, and declare them for yourself in your own voice. Give each line time to sink in.

Massimo's Declaration
(with appreciation to Bob Dunham)

I am a human being.
I am only a human being.
I'm not superman or superwoman.
I'm not perfect.
Perfection is only a story good for suffering,
And I've been living that story for my whole life.
But now I see that
It's just my story,

And I can be the author of my story
Rather than a victim of it.
This old story
Is just an echo of an old conversation
That got trapped in my nervous system
And has been haunting me ever since.
But it's not the truth.
It's just a story.
I'm not a machine.
I am a human being,
And human beings are finite.
I can't know everything.
I can't do everything.
I can't please everybody.
But I can do a lot.
I can make invitations.
I can make requests.
I can make offers.
I can produce action with others
To create a shared future that we care about
And make it happen.
That's pretty frickin' amazing.
And so I hereby declare a new story:
That I am a human being,
And that is enough.
Thanks to Life.

CONCLUSION
Finding Your Way Home

Fall 2020, Lopez Island, Washington State Coast

I sat on a large rock by the ocean, watching the sun set over the horizon with a rare green flash. This elusive phenomenon is caused when a mirage and sunlight dispersion combine. The rarity of the moment aligned both internally and with my external surroundings.

I'd come to beautiful Lopez Island for a solo retreat hosted by my executive coach, Abigail. She invited me for a ceremony to unpack my metaphorical baggage and only repack the pieces I wanted to carry with me as I moved into a new beginning and the next chapter of my career. I wasn't there yet. It had been only a few weeks since I had been let go from my job at Slalom, after taking a leave of absence in the wake of my panic attack.

I was in the middle phase of what William Bridges's book *Transitions* considers the three phases of change: Ending,

Neutral Zone, and New Beginning.[81] Abigail encouraged me to look back with courage and curiosity so that I wouldn't get stuck in the past of being hurt, hurting others, and considering myself a failure. I chose to step into the Neutral Zone to accept that the job was now in the past and nothing could be done about it, but the lessons I was meant to learn from it were front and center.

When I arrived on Lopez Island, Abigail walked me through the ceremony I'd be conducting on my own after dark. I set the intention to learn from the experience that had left me shattered. I would look at everything I'd been carrying and then selectively choose the pieces to put myself back together and step into the future with integrity and self-compassion.

Once she left, I settled into the space. I stared in awe at the glassy pond, ringed with a path and tall grasses—concentric circles with an endless sky above. The property, located on the southwest tip of the island, was a ten-minute walk from the beach, so I made my way there to watch the sun go down.

I listened to the birds, the wind, and the water, and took time to meditate. After the gorgeous sunset, I walked back to the campsite and built a fire. The process of the ceremony touched on all the directions I explored in this book. I looked inward, outward, backward, forward, leeward, and windward. I reread all the journal entries I had made since my panic attack. As I read each page out loud, I tossed the pages into the fire. I had taken what I needed, and I let the rest go.

That night I sat quietly under the stars and felt a lightness for the first time in months. I felt clarity that I had what I needed within me to move forward. I was overcome by a sense of joy and gratitude that I get to live this life, no matter how hard it can be at times. I felt a sense of appreciation for myself, my resilience, and the courage I had summoned to be honest and take responsibility for my life and career. I slept deeply and peacefully under the starry sky and woke to the morning light feeling renewed physically, mentally, emotionally, and spiritually. That night was one of the pivotal moments that led me toward my new life and to documenting what I've learned in this book.

I began a daily practice of self-compassion. I allowed myself to feel lonely and then asked for help and shared my experience. I was mindfully aware of my emotions and allowed feelings to wash over me, not with judgment but with curiosity about what they might teach me. I treated myself with kindness by taking the time to heal while holding myself accountable to take action on what I've learned along the way so I can step boldly into the New Beginning. It's been a few years now, and I'm still practicing, still learning, still unpacking, and repacking. I'll never be finished.

There was never a monster or villain in my story in the form of another person or organization. At the core of it all, I was always waging my own internal war with insecurity. It is only through my practice of self-compassion that I keep the monster at bay when it returns for battle. But just like my well-intentioned, misinformed protectors (WIMPs), the roommates I can't evict, my battles with internal demons have proven to be the richest experiences, fertile soil for evolution and growth.

I got my first taste of the transformative power of self-compassion during the Hoffman Process, discussed in the introduction. Over the first few days, I felt a slow but consistent release of my old thinking and behavioral patterns. A lighter, gentler, kinder voice emerged in place of my WIMPs. One afternoon, after a guided visualization meditation, I went for a walk. As I strolled down a tree-lined road and the sun hit my face, I experienced a feeling of euphoria and spontaneously burst into laughter. I'm not talking about a quiet chuckle, but a deep belly laugh that shook my entire body. It was the kind of exuberant, carefree laugh we adore in children but rarely experience as adults. I couldn't contain myself. Laughing so hard only made me laugh more. A gushing faucet of unfiltered joy was spilling out and washing over me as raucous laughter, pure self-love, and acceptance.

I have never felt anything like it before or since.

I know love and loss, joy and despair, failure and triumph. I don't have to read about these human experiences because I've lived through them. The full breadth and depth of being human helps us empathize, tap into our resilience, and broaden our emotional fluency. As Robin Williams's character explains to Matt Damon's in the movie *Good Will Hunting*,

> If I asked you about art you could give me the skinny on
> every art book ever written . . . but you couldn't tell me what
> it smells like in the Sistine Chapel. You've never stood there
> and looked up at that beautiful ceiling. . . . And if I asked
> you about love I'd get a sonnet, but you've never looked at
> a woman and been truly vulnerable. . . . You wouldn't know
> about sleeping sitting up in a hospital room for two months
> holding her hand and not leaving because the doctors could
> see in your eyes that the term "visiting hours" didn't apply
> to you. And you wouldn't know about real loss, because that

only occurs when you lose something you love more than yourself, and you've never dared to love anything that much.

Experiencing it all, the beauty and pain, is what makes me feel alive. I no longer hold resentment about what happened *to me* but deep gratitude for what happened *for me*. I still don't like *how* it happened, but I appreciate that it served as the kick in the ass I needed to do what I'd been afraid to do for too long: be who I truly am at my core and fully claim my life.

My goal on this path and with this book is to share my story of giving up on being better than everyone else and instead being fully myself. There is not just one way to do this. Find what works for you.

You can't go wrong if you trust what feels right for you.

NOTES

INTRODUCTION

1. Dan Harris, "The Benefits of Not Being a Jerk to Yourself @TED #shorts," YouTube video, November 21, 2022, www.youtube.com /watch?v=ZAa-ozcaP_0.

2. Kristin Neff, *Self-Compassion: The Proven Power of Being Kind to Yourself* (New York: HarperCollins, 2011).

3. Laura K. Barnard and John F. Curry, "Self-Compassion: Conceptualizations, Correlates, and Interventions," *Review of General Psychology* 15, no. 4 (2011): 289–303, https://doi.org/10.1037 /a0025754.

4. Ibid.

1. THE TWO JOBS

5. Robert Kegan and Lisa Laskow Lahey, *Immunity to Change: How to Overcome It and Unlock Potential in Yourself and Your Organization* (Boston: Harvard Business Press, 2009).

6. Robert Kegan, Lisa Laskow Lahey, and Matthew L. Miller, *An Everyone Culture: Becoming a Deliberately Developmental Organization* (Boston: Harvard Business Review Press, 2016).

7. Zeena Hashem and Pia Zeinoun, "Self-Compassion Explains Less Burnout among Healthcare Professionals," *Mindfulness* 11, no. 11 (2020): 2542–2551, https://doi.org/10.1007/s12671-020-01469-5.

8. Howard Stern and Jon Stewart, "Jon Stewart on His Early Days Doing Stand-Up," *The Howard Stern Show*, YouTube video, published January 29, 2023, https://www.youtube.com/watch?v= UzvsuDLmtFE.

9. Richard C. Schwartz, *Unburdening the Self: The Promise of Internal Family Systems Therapy* (Boulder, CO: Sounds True, 2019).

10. Kegan and Lahey, *Immunity to Change.*

11. Tara Brach, *Trusting the Gold: Uncovering Your Natural Goodness* (Boulder, CO: Sounds True, 2021).

12. Yuval N. Harari, John Purcell, and Haim Watzman, *Sapiens: A Brief History of Humankind* (New York: Harper Perennial, 2018).

13. Ibid.

2. ZERO-FLUFF ZONE

14. Iya Gana Aliyu, Yusuf Ismail, and Mukhtar Alhaji Liman, "The Taxonomy of Educational Objectives: An Evaluation of the Learning Domains," *Sokoto Educational Review* 14, no. 1 (June 2013): 121–130.

15. Tasha Eurich, *Insight: The Surprising Truth about How Others See Us, How We See Ourselves, and Why the Answers Matter More Than We Think* (New York: Currency, 2018).

16. Rory Vaden, "Buffalo Charge the Storm Story," August 17, 2020, YouTube video, https://www.youtube.com/watch?v= azcS1SXoQeA&t=8s.

17. Phoebe Long, "Make Self-Compassion One of Your New Year's Resolutions," *Greater Good*, January 3, 2018, https://greatergood .berkeley.edu/article/item/make_self_compassion_one_of_your_new _years_resolutions.

18. Juliana G. Breines and Serena Chen, "Self-Compassion Increases Self-Improvement Motivation," *Personality and Social Psychology Bulletin* 38, no. 9 (2012): 1133–1143, https://doi.org/10.1177 /0146167212445599.

19. Lynn R. Offermann and Kira Foley, "Is There a Female Leadership Advantage?" in *Oxford Research Encyclopedia of Business and Management* (2020), https://doi.org/10.1093/acrefore /9780190224851.013.61.

20. "Measuring the Return on Character," *Harvard Business Review*, April 1, 2015, https://hbr.org/2015/04/measuring-the-return -on-character.

21. Y. Joel Wong, Moon-Ho Ringo Ho, Shu-Yi Wang, and I. S. Miller, "Meta-Analyses of the Relationship between Conformity to Masculine Norms and Mental Health-Related Outcomes," *Journal of Counseling Psychology* 64, no. 1 (2017): 80–93, https://doi.org/10.1037/cou0000176.

22. Matthew F. Garnett and Sally C. Curtin, "Suicide Mortality in the United States, 2001–2021," NCHS Data Brief no. 464 (Hyattsville, MD: National Center for Health Statistics, 2023), https://www.cdc.gov/nchs/products/databriefs/db464.htm.

3. THE WARD MODEL

23. Barry Johnson, *Polarity Management: Identifying and Managing Unsolvable Problems* (Amherst, MA: HRD Press, 2014).

24. Nate Regier, *Compassionate Accountability: How Leaders Build Connection and Get Results* (Oakland, CA: Berrett-Koehler Publishers, 2023).

4. AWARENESS

25. Glennon Doyle, *Untamed* (New York: Dial Press, 2020).

26. Bonnie Hayden Cheng and Julie M. McCarthy, "Understanding the Dark and Bright Sides of Anxiety: A Theory of Workplace Anxiety," *Journal of Applied Psychology* 103, no. 5 (2018): 537–560, https://doi.org/10.1037/apl0000266.

27. Dawn Klinghoffer and Katie Kirkpatrick-Husk, "More Than 50% of Managers Feel Burned Out," *Harvard Business Review*, May 18, 2023.

28. Mika Kivimäki and Ichiro Kawachi, "Work Stress As a Risk Factor for Cardiovascular Disease," *Current Cardiology Reports* 17, no. 9 (2015), https://doi.org/10.1007/s11886-015-0630-8.

29. Marc Fadel, Grace Sembajwe, Diana Gagliardi, Fernando Pico, Jian Li, Anna Ozguler, et al., "Association between Reported Long Working Hours and History of Stroke in the CONSTANCES Cohort," *Stroke* 50, no. 7 (2019): 1879–1882, https://doi.org/10.1161/strokeaha.119.025454.

30. Jean Madigan, *Thinking on Your Feet* (Richardson, TX: Action Based Learning, 2000).

31. Ibid.

32. Eric Jensen and Liesl McConchie, *Brain-Based Learning: The New Paradigm of Teaching* (Thousand Oaks, CA: Corwin Press, 2020).

33. Will Bulsiewicz, *Fiber Fueled: The Plant-Based Gut Health Program for Losing Weight, Restoring Your Health, and Optimizing Your Microbiome* (New York: Avery, 2020).

34. Eric Suni, "How Much Sleep Do We Really Need?" Sleep Foundation, April 13, 2022, https://www.sleepfoundation.org/how-sleep-works/how-much-sleep-do-we-really-need.

35. Debra Trampe, Jordi Quoidbach, and Maxime Taquet, "Emotions in Everyday Life," *PLOS ONE* 10, no. 12 (2015), https://doi.org/10.1371/journal.pone.0145450.

36. Susan David, *Emotional Agility: Get Unstuck, Embrace Change, and Thrive in Work and Life* (New York: Penguin, 2016).

37. Brené Brown, Nicholas Saldivar, and Paul Dugdale, directors, *Brené Brown: Atlas of the Heart* (Den of Thieves, 2022).

38. Daniel Goleman, *Emotional Intelligence* (New York: Bantam Books, 2007).

39. David, *Emotional Agility*.

40. Daniel M. Wegner and David J. Schneider, "The White Bear Story," *Psychological Inquiry* 14, no. 3/4 (2003): 326–329, http://www.jstor.org/stable/1449696.

41. Alex Lieberman, "Why Alexis Ohanian Left Reddit to Build an Impact-Focused VC Firm," *Imposters*, July 5, 2022, podcast audio, https://imposters.morningbrew.com/why-alexis-ohanian-left-reddit-to-build-an-impact-focused-vc-firm/.

42. Timothy D. Wilson, David A. Reinhard, Erin C. Westgate, Daniel T. Gilbert, Nicole Ellerbeck, Cheryl Hahn, et al., "Just Think: The Challenges of the Disengaged Mind," *Science* 345, no. 6192 (2014): 75–77, https://doi.org/10.1126/science.1250830.

43. Adam M. Grant, *Think Again: The Power of Knowing What You Don't Know* (New York: Viking, 2021).

44. Matthew A. Killingsworth and Daniel T. Gilbert, "A Wandering Mind Is an Unhappy Mind," *Science* 330, no. 6006 (2010):

932, https://www.science.org/doi/10.1126/science.1192439?url_ver
=Z39.88-2003&rfr_id=ori:rid:crossref.org&rfr_dat=cr_pub%20
%20pubmed.

  45. Neff, *Self-Compassion.*

  46. A.L. Dueren, A. Vafeiadou, C. Edgar, and M. J. Banissy,
"The Influence of Duration, Arm Crossing Style, Gender, and
Emotional Closeness on Hugging Behaviour," *Acta Psychologica*
221 (2021): 103441, https://www.sciencedirect.com/science/article/pii
/S0001691821001918?via%3Dihub.

5. ACCEPTANCE

  47. Neff, *Self-Compassion.*

  48. David Goggins, *Can't Hurt Me: Master Your Mind and Defy the
Odds* (Austin, TX: Lioncrest, 2020).

  49. Gallup, *State of the Global Workplace 2022 Report* (Washington,
DC: Gallup, 2022), p. 4, https://www.gallup.com/workplace/349484
/state-of-the-global-workplace-2022-report.aspx.

  50. Jon Kabat-Zinn, *Wherever You Go, There You Are: Mindfulness
Meditation for Everyday Life* (London: Piatkus, 2016).

  51. William Bridges, *Transitions: Making Sense of Life's Changes*
(Boston: Da Capo Lifelong, 2020).

6. ACCOUNTABILITY

  52. Iona Holloway, "Brave Thing," accessed January 9, 2024,
https://www.bravething.co/.

  53. Amanda McCracken, "How to Love Yourself for Real,
According to Therapists," *Self*, March 4, 2022, https://www.self.com
/story/how-to-love-yourself.

  54. Xue Wang, Zhansheng Chen, Kai-Tak Poon, Fei Teng, and
Shenghua Jin, "Self-Compassion Decreases Acceptance of Own
Immoral Behaviors," *Personality and Individual Differences* 106
(February 1, 2017): 329–333, https://doi.org/10.1016/j.paid.2016.10.030.

  55. Kristin Neff, "Self-Compassion Practices: Tips for Practice,"
Self-Compassion, accessed January 6, 2024, https://self-compassion
.org/tips-for-practice/.

56. Sigal Samuel, "Self-Compassion Isn't Just Trendy, It's a Real Way to Manage Shame, Anxiety, and Depression," *Vox*, August 2, 2022, https://www.vox.com/even-better/23274105/self-compassion -shame-anxiety-depression.

57. Joseph Goldstein, *The Experience of Insight: A Natural Unfolding* (Kandy, Sri Lanka: Buddhist Publication Society, 2008).

58. Neff, "Self-Compassion Practices: Tips for Practice."

59. Kristin Neff, *Fierce Self-Compassion: How Women Can Harness Kindness to Speak Up, Claim Their Power, and Thrive* (New York: HarperWave, 2021).

7. PERFECTLY IMPERFECT

60. Grant, *Think Again*.

61. Ibid.

62. Ibid.

63. Yasuhiro Kotera and William Van Gordon, "Effects of Self-Compassion Training on Work-Related Well-Being: A Systematic Review," *Frontiers in Psychology* 12 (2021), https://doi.org/10.3389 /fpsyg.2021.630798.

64. Michael Bungay Stanier, *The Coaching Habit* (Toronto: Box of Crayons Press, 2016).

65. Brené Brown, *Dare to Lead: Brave Work, Tough Conversations, Whole Hearts* (New York: Random House, 2018).

66. Elizabeth Grace Saunders, "To Reach Your Goals, Embrace Self-Compassion," *Harvard Business Review*, February 22, 2022, https://hbr.org/2022/02/to-reach-your-goals-embrace-self -compassion.

67. Scott Shute, *The Full Body Yes: Change Your Work and Your World from the Inside Out* (Vancouver, BC: Page Two Books, 2021).

68. Dan Sullivan, *The Gap and the Gain: The High Achievers' Guide to Happiness, Confidence, and Success* (Carlsbad, CA: Hay House, 2021).

8. RIPPLE EFFECT

69. Mark Manson, "The Backwards Law," Mark Manson, accessed October 20, 2023, https://markmanson.net/the-backwards -law.

70. Marshall Goldsmith and Mark Reiter, *What Got You Here Won't Get You There: How Successful People Become Even More Successful!* (New York: Hachette Go, 2020).

71. Philip Brickman and Donald T. Campbell, "Hedonic Relativism and Planning the Good Society," in *Adaptation-Level Theory: A Symposium*, ed. Michael H. Appley, 287–302 (New York: Academic Press, 1971).

72. Rasmus Hougaard and Jacqueline Carter, *The Mind of the Leader: How to Lead Yourself, Your People, and Your Organization for Extraordinary Results* (Boston: Harvard Business Review Press, 2018).

73. Julie Winkle Giulioni, *Promotions Are So Yesterday* (Alexandria, VA: ATD Press, 2022).

74. Kotera and Van Gordon, "Effects of Self-Compassion Training on Work-Related Well-Being."

75. Mary Hayes, Frances Chumney, and Marcus Buckingham, *Global Workplace Study 2020* (Roseland, NJ: ADP Research Institute, 2020), https://www.adpri.org/research/global-workplace-study/.

76. Keith McCandless and Henri Lipmanowicz, "Troika Consulting," Liberating Structures, accessed November 27, 2023, https://www.liberatingstructures.com/8-troika-consulting/.

77. Marcos Cajina Heinzkill and Gregory Stebbins, "Self-Compassion: The Doorway to Wise Leadership," LinkedIn, April 15, 2015, https://www.linkedin.com/pulse/sustainable-leadership -through-wisdom-compassion-stebbins-ed-d-/.

78. Caitlin A. Orsini and Nicholas W. Simon, "Reward/ Punishment-Based Decision Making in Rodents," *Current Protocols in Neuroscience* 93, no. 1 (2020), https://doi.org/10.1002/cpns.100.

79. Breines and Chen, "Self-Compassion Increases Self-Improvement Motivation."

80. Mitchell Green, "Speech Acts," *The Stanford Encyclopedia of Philosophy* (Fall 2021 Edition), ed. Edward N. Zalta, https://plato.stanford.edu/archives/fall2021/entries/speech-acts/.

CONCLUSION

81. Bridges, *Transitions.*

BIBLIOGRAPHY

Aliyu, Iya Gana, Yusuf Ismail, and Mukhtar Alhaji Liman. "The Taxonomy of Educational Objectives: An Evaluation of the Learning Domains." *Sokoto Educational Review* 14, no. 1 (June 2013): 121–130.

Ankney, Douglas. "Correlation Between Dyslexia and Criminal Behavior; First Step Act to Require Screening, Treatment." *Prison Legal News*, August 6, 2019. https://www.prisonlegalnews.org /news/2019/aug/6/correlation-between-dyslexia-and-criminal -behavior-first-step-act-require-screening-treatment/.

Barnard, Laura K., and John F. Curry. "Self-Compassion: Conceptualizations, Correlates, and Interventions." *Review of General Psychology*, 15, no. 4 (2011): 289–303. https://doi.org/10.1037 /a0025754.

Brach, Tara. *Trusting the Gold: Uncovering Your Natural Goodness.* Boulder, CO: Sounds True, 2021.

Breines, Juliana G., and Serena Chen. "Self-Compassion Increases Self-Improvement Motivation." *Personality and Social Psychology Bulletin* 38, no. 9 (2012): 1133–1143. https://doi.org/10.1177 /0146167212445599.

Brickman, Philip, and Donald T. Campbell. "Hedonic Relativism and Planning the Good Society." In *Adaptation-Level Theory: A Symposium*, ed. Michael H. Appley, 287–302. New York: Academic Press, 1971.

Bridges, William. *Transitions: Making Sense of Life's Changes.* Boston: Da Capo Lifelong, 2020.

Brown, Brené. *Dare to Lead: Brave Work, Tough Conversations, Whole Hearts*. New York: Random House, 2018.

Brown, Brené, Nicholas Saldivar, and Paul Dugdale, directors. *Brené Brown: Atlas of the Heart*. Den of Thieves, 2022.

Bulsiewicz, Will. *Fiber Fueled: The Plant-Based Gut Health Program for Losing Weight, Restoring Your Health, and Optimizing Your Microbiome*. New York: Avery, 2020.

Cajina Heinzkill, Marcos, and Gregory Stebbins. "Self-Compassion: The Doorway to Wise Leadership." LinkedIn, April 15, 2015.

Cheng, Bonnie Hayden, and Julie M. McCarthy. "Understanding the Dark and Bright Sides of Anxiety: A Theory of Workplace Anxiety." *Journal of Applied Psychology* 103, no. 5 (2018): 537–560. https://doi.org/10.1037/apl0000266.

Clark, Dorie, and Christie Smith. "Help Your Employees Be Themselves at Work." *Harvard Business Review*, November 3, 2014. https://hbr.org/2014/11/help-your-employees-be-themselves-at-work.

David, Susan. *Emotional Agility: Get Unstuck, Embrace Change, and Thrive in Work and Life*. New York: Penguin, 2016.

Doyle, Glennon. *Untamed*. New York: Dial Press, 2020.

Dueren A.L., A. Vafeiadou, C. Edgar, and M. J. Banissy. "The Influence of Duration, Arm Crossing Style, Gender, and Emotional Closeness on Hugging Behaviour." *Acta Psychologica* 221 (2021): 103441. https://www.sciencedirect.com/science/article/pii/S0001691821001918?via%3Dihub.

Eurich, Tasha. *Insight: The Surprising Truth about How Others See Us, How We See Ourselves, and Why the Answers Matter More Than We Think*. New York: Currency, 2018.

Fadel, Marc, Grace Sembajwe, Diana Gagliardi, Fernando Pico, Jian Li, Anna Ozguler, et al. "Association between Reported Long Working Hours and History of Stroke in the CONSTANCES Cohort." *Stroke* 50, no. 7 (2019): 1879–1882. https://doi.org/10.1161/strokeaha.119.025454.

Gallup. *State of the Global Workplace 2022 Report*. Washington, DC: Gallup, 2022. https://www.gallup.com/workplace/349484/state-of-the-global-workplace-2022-report.aspx.

Garnett, Matthew F., and Sally C. Curtin. "Suicide Mortality in the United States, 2001–2021." NCHS Data Brief no. 464. Hyattsville, MD: National Center for Health Statistics, 2023. https://www.cdc.gov/nchs/products/databriefs/db464.htm.

Giulioni, Julie Winkle. *Promotions Are So Yesterday*. Alexandria, VA: ATD Press, 2022.

Goggins, David. *Can't Hurt Me: Master Your Mind and Defy the Odds*. Austin, TX: Lioncrest, 2020.

Goldsmith, Marshall, and Mark Reiter. *What Got You Here Won't Get You There: How Successful People Become Even More Successful!* New York: Hachette Go, 2020.

Goleman, Daniel. *Emotional Intelligence*. New York: Bantam Books, 2007.

Grant, Adam M. *Think Again: The Power of Knowing What You Don't Know*. New York: Viking, 2021.

Green, Mitchell. "Speech Acts." *The Stanford Encyclopedia of Philosophy* (Fall 2021 Edition), ed. Edward N. Zalta. https://plato.stanford.edu/archives/fall2021/entries/speech-acts/.

Gross, Alex Lieberman. "Why Alexis Ohanian Left Reddit to Build an Impact-Focused VC Firm." *Imposters*, July 5, 2022. Podcast audio. https://imposters.morningbrew.com/why-alexis-ohanian-left-reddit-to-build-an-impact-focused-vc-firm/.

Harari, Yuval N., John Purcell, and Haim Watzman. *Sapiens: A Brief History of Humankind*. New York: Harper Perennial, 2018.

Harris, Dan. "The Benefits of Not Being a Jerk to Yourself @TED #shorts." YouTube video, November 21, 2022. www.youtube.com/watch?v=ZAa-ozcaP_0.

Hashem, Zeena, and Pia Zeinoun. "Self-Compassion Explains Less Burnout among Healthcare Professionals." *Mindfulness* 11, no. 11 (2020): 2542–2551. https://doi.org/10.1007/s12671-020-01469-5.

Hayes, Mary, Frances Chumney, and Marcus Buckingham. *Global Workplace Study 2020*. Roseland, NJ: ADP Research Institute, 2020. https://www.adpri.org/research/global-workplace-study/.

Holloway, Iona. "Brave Thing." Accessed January 9, 2024. https://www.bravething.co/.

Hougaard, Rasmus, and Jacqueline Carter. *The Mind of the Leader: How to Lead Yourself, Your People, and Your Organization for Extraordinary Results.* Boston: Harvard Business Review Press, 2018.

Jensen, Eric, and Liesl McConchie. *Brain-Based Learning: The New Paradigm of Teaching.* Thousand Oaks, CA: Corwin Press, 2020.

Johnson, Barry. *Polarity Management: Identifying and Managing Unsolvable Problems.* Amherst, MA: HRD Press, 2014.

Kabat-Zinn, Jon. *Wherever You Go, There You Are: Mindfulness Meditation for Everyday Life.* London: Piatkus, 2016.

Kegan, Robert, and Lisa Laskow Lahey. *Immunity to Change: How to Overcome It and Unlock Potential in Yourself and Your Organization.* Boston: Harvard Business Review Press, 2009.

Kegan, Robert, Lisa Laskow Lahey, and Matthew L. Miller. *An Everyone Culture: Becoming a Deliberately Developmental Organization.* Boston: Harvard Business Review Press, 2016.

Killingsworth, Matthew A., and Daniel T. Gilbert. "A Wandering Mind Is an Unhappy Mind." *Science* 330, no. 6006 (2010): 932. https://www.science.org/doi/10.1126/science.1192439?url_ver= Z39.88-2003&rfr_id=ori:rid:crossref.org&rfr_dat=cr_pub%20 %20pubmed.

Kivimäki, Mika, and Ichiro Kawachi. "Work Stress As a Risk Factor for Cardiovascular Disease." *Current Cardiology Reports* 17, no. 9 (2015). https://doi.org/10.1007/s11886-015-0630-8.

Klinghoffer, Dawn, and Katie Kirkpatrick-Husk. "More Than 50% of Managers Feel Burned Out." *Harvard Business Review* (May 2023). https://hbr.org/2023/05/more-than-50-of-managers-feel -burned-out.

Kotera, Yasuhiro, and William Van Gordon. "Effects of Self-Compassion Training on Work-Related Well-Being: A Systematic Review." *Frontiers in Psychology* 12 (April 23, 2021). https://doi.org /10.3389/fpsyg.2021.630798.

Long, Phoebe. "Make Self-Compassion One of Your New Year's Resolutions." Greater Good, January 3, 2018. https://greatergood .berkeley.edu/article/item/make_self_compassion_one_of_your _new_years_resolutions.

Madigan, Jean. *Thinking on Your Feet*. Richardson, TX: Action Based Learning, 2000.

Manson, Mark. "The Backwards Law." Mark Manson. Accessed October 20, 2023. https://markmanson.net/the-backwards-law.

McCandless, Keith, and Henri Lipmanowic. "Troika Consulting." Liberating Structures. Accessed November 27, 2023. https://www.liberatingstructures.com/8-troika-consulting/.

McCracken, Amanda. "How to Love Yourself for Real, According to Therapists." *Self*, March 4, 2022. https://www.self.com/story/how-to-love-yourself.

"Measuring the Return on Character." *Harvard Business Review*, April 1, 2015. https://hbr.org/2015/04/measuring-the-return-on-character.

Neff, Kristin. *Fierce Self-Compassion: How Women Can Harness Kindness to Speak up, Claim Their Power, and Thrive*. New York: HarperWave, 2021.

Neff, Kristin. *Self-Compassion: The Proven Power of Being Kind to Yourself*. New York: HarperCollins, 2011.

Neff, Kristin. "Self-Compassion Practices: Tips for Practice." Self-Compassion. Accessed January 6, 2024. https://self-compassion.org/tips-for-practice/.

Offermann, Lynn R., and Kira Foley. "Is There a Female Leadership Advantage?" *Oxford Research Encyclopedia of Business and Management*, 2020. https://doi.org/10.1093/acrefore/9780190224851.013.61.

Orsini, Caitlin A., and Nicholas W. Simon. "Reward/Punishment-Based Decision Making in Rodents." *Current Protocols in Neuroscience* 93, no. 1 (2020): e100. https://doi.org/10.1002/cpns.100.

Regier, Nate. *Compassionate Accountability: How Leaders Build Connection and Get Results*. Oakland, CA: Berrett-Koehler Publishers, 2023.

Samuel, Sigal. "Self-Compassion Isn't Just Trendy, It's a Real Way to Manage Shame, Anxiety, and Depression." *Vox*, August 2, 2022. https://www.vox.com/even-better/23274105/self-compassion-shame-anxiety-depression.

Saunders, Elizabeth Grace. "To Reach Your Goals, Embrace Self-Compassion." *Harvard Business Review*, February 22, 2022. https://hbr.org/2022/02/to-reach-your-goals-embrace-self -compassion.

Schwartz, Richard C. *Unburdening the Self: The Promise of Internal Family Systems Therapy*. Boulder, CO: Sounds True, 2019.

Shute, Scott. *The Full Body Yes: Change Your Work and Your World from the Inside Out*. Vancouver, BC: Page Two Books, 2021.

Stanier, Bungay Michael. *The Coaching Habit*. Toronto: Box of Crayons Press, 2016.

Stern, Howard, and Jon Stewart. "Jon Stewart on His Early Days Doing Stand-Up." *The Howard Stern Show*. YouTube video, January 29, 2023. https://www.youtube.com/watch?v=Uzvsu DLmtFE.

Sullivan, Dan. *Gap and the Gain: The High Achievers' Guide to Happiness, Confidence, and Success*. Carlsbad, CA: Hay House, 2021.

Suni, Eric. "How Much Sleep Do We Really Need?" Sleep Foundation, April 13, 2022. https://www.sleepfoundation.org/how -sleep-works/how-much-sleep-do-we-really-need.

Trampe, Debra, Jordi Quoidbach, and Maxime Taquet. "Emotions in Everyday Life." *PLOS ONE* 10, no. 12 (2015). https://doi.org/10.1371 /journal.pone.0145450.

Vaden, Rory. "Buffalo Charge the Storm Story." YouTube video, August 17, 2020. https://www.youtube.com/watch?v=azcS1SXoQeA &t=8s.

Wang, Xue, Zhansheng Chen, Kai-Tak Poon, Fei Teng, and Shenghua Jin. "Self-Compassion Decreases Acceptance of Own Immoral Behaviors." *Personality and Individual Differences* 106 (February 1, 2017): 329–333. https://doi.org/10.1016/j.paid.2016.10.030.

Wegner, Daniel M., and David J. Schneider. "The White Bear Story." *Psychological Inquiry* 14, no. 3/4 (2003): 326–329. http://www.jstor .org/stable/1449696.

Wilson, Timothy D., David A. Reinhard, Erin C. Westgate, Daniel T. Gilbert, Nicole Ellerbeck, Cheryl Hahn, et al. "Just Think: The

Challenges of the Disengaged Mind." *Science* 345, no. 6192 (2014): 75–77. https://doi.org/10.1126/science.1250830.

Wong, Y. Joel, Moon-Ho Ringo Ho, Shu-Yi Wang, and I. S. Miller. "Meta-Analyses of the Relationship between Conformity to Masculine Norms and Mental Health-Related Outcomes." *Journal of Counseling Psychology* 64, no. 1 (2017): 80–93. https://doi.org/10.1037/cou0000176.

ACKNOWLEDGMENTS

In the final pages of this book, I am compelled to express my deepest gratitude and acknowledge those who have been pillars of strength, inspiration, and support throughout this journey.

To my beloved wife, Brie Backus: Without your unwavering love, support, and belief in me, the journey to this book's completion would have been unimaginable. You have been my sanctuary when venturing into the darkest parts of myself, illuminating the beauty and potential of life. You are nothing short of a miracle in my life.

To my son, Luca: The love I have for you is boundless. You are the embodiment of my greatest joy and have expanded my heart in ways I never knew possible. My dearest hope is that this book serves as a beacon for you, guiding you to chase your dreams, whatever they may be, with the same fervor and passion that you've awakened in me.

To my parents, John and Valerie Backus: Your endless love, generosity, and belief have been the bedrock of my courage and determination. You have provided me with more than a son could ever wish for—the strength to dream and the means to chase those dreams.

To Juliane Bergmann: Your patience, wisdom, curiosity,

honesty, and unwavering loyalty to this project have been a guiding light. I am eternally grateful for your guidance and confidence in me, and I eagerly wait for the world to discover the remarkable person you are, as I have.

To Robb Gilbear and Moriah Bacus: In times when despair seemed inevitable, you were the lifelines that kept me afloat. Your support has been invaluable.

To John Powers: Your guidance through the darkest times has been a beacon, consistently leading me back home. Your wisdom and insight have been indispensable.

To the Hoffman Institute: Your teachings, community, and processes have not only inspired this book but also profoundly transformed the way I live, love, and lead. Your influence is immeasurable.

To all my past and present clients: Witnessing your courage to let go of the burden of self-protection in favor of leading with self-compassion has been the greatest honor of my professional life. Experiencing the best of who you are has been a source of endless inspiration and humility.

Each of you has played an integral role in this journey, and for that, my gratitude knows no bounds.

INDEX

Entries that have a page number followed by *f* reference a figure.

ABOUT THE AUTHOR

Massimo Backus is a distinguished executive coach and leadership development consultant who has worked with more than 3,000 leaders from Amazon, Cisco, Salesforce, United Healthcare, Sony, Nintendo, and Fox Entertainment. He holds a BA in psychology from Seattle University, an MA in organizational behavior psychology from Claremont Graduate University, and certifications including the Lominger Leadership Architect, DISC, MBTI, and Hogan Assessment Systems.

He is known for designing specialized programs to tackle leadership effectiveness, team dynamics, and organizational culture. His coaching methodology, grounded in leadership science, behavioral change, and self-compassion, enhances emotional intelligence, adaptability, and resilience in leaders who create thriving, sustainable, and highly successful organizations.

Massimo serves on the board of Hamlin Robinson School

in Seattle to further the academic and creative potential of students with dyslexia and other language-based learning differences. He grew up in the Pacific Northwest and lives in Seattle with his wife and son.

Berrett–Koehler
Publishers

Berrett-Koehler is an independent publisher dedicated to an ambitious mission: *Connecting people and ideas to create a world that works for all.*

Our publications span many formats, including print, digital, audio, and video. We also offer online resources, training, and gatherings. And we will continue expanding our products and services to advance our mission.

We believe that the solutions to the world's problems will come from all of us, working at all levels: in our society, in our organizations, and in our own lives. Our publications and resources offer pathways to creating a more just, equitable, and sustainable society. They help people make their organizations more humane, democratic, diverse, and effective (and we don't think there's any contradiction there). And they guide people in creating positive change in their own lives and aligning their personal practices with their aspirations for a better world.

And we strive to practice what we preach through what we call "The BK Way." At the core of this approach is *stewardship,* a deep sense of responsibility to administer the company for the benefit of all of our stakeholder groups, including authors, customers, employees, investors, service providers, sales partners, and the communities and environment around us. Everything we do is built around stewardship and our other core values of *quality, partnership, inclusion,* and *sustainability.*

This is why Berrett-Koehler is the first book publishing company to be both a B Corporation (a rigorous certification) and a benefit corporation (a for-profit legal status), which together require us to adhere to the highest standards for corporate, social, and environmental performance. And it is why we have instituted many pioneering practices (which you can learn about at www.bkconnection.com), including the Berrett-Koehler Constitution, the Bill of Rights and Responsibilities for BK Authors, and our unique Author Days.

We are grateful to our readers, authors, and other friends who are supporting our mission. We ask you to share with us examples of how BK publications and resources are making a difference in your lives, organizations, and communities at www.bkconnection.com/impact.

Dear reader,

Thank you for picking up this book and welcome to the worldwide BK community! You're joining a special group of people who have come together to create positive change in their lives, organizations, and communities.

What's BK all about?

Our mission is to connect people and ideas to create a world that works for all.

Why? Our communities, organizations, and lives get bogged down by old paradigms of self-interest, exclusion, hierarchy, and privilege. But we believe that can change. That's why we seek the leading experts on these challenges—and share their actionable ideas with you.

A welcome gift

To help you get started, we'd like to offer you a **free copy** of one of our bestselling ebooks:

www.bkconnection.com/welcome

When you claim your **free ebook**, you'll also be subscribed to our blog.

Our freshest insights

Access the best new tools and ideas for leaders at all levels on our blog at ideas.bkconnection.com.

Sincerely,

Your friends at Berrett-Koehler

Certified

Corporation